D0209469

The Genesis of a Novel

THOMAS MANN

The Genesis of a Novel

TRANSLATED FROM THE GERMAN BY
Richard and Clara Winston

London
SECKER & WARBURG

At the time of its publication every work of fancy should stand upon its own feet and accomplish its own effect. Hence I have never been fond of supplementing any of mine with prefaces or postscripts, nor have I offered any apologies to the critics. Nevertheless, the more such works recede into the past, the more ineffective they become, in measure to their effectiveness at the moment. Indeed, they are the less esteemed, the more thay have bestowed upon the country's culture, as mothers are so easily overshadowed by a bevy of beautiful daughters. Therefore it is meet and fitting to win for them their historical value by discussing their origins with men of understanding and good will.

GOETHE, *Poetry and Truth*

THOMAS MANN

I

DIARY ENTRIES FOR 1945 SHOW ME THAT ON DECEMBER 22 of that year the Los Angeles correspondent of *Time* called on me (it is an hour's drive from downtown Los Angeles to our country home). He came to challenge me concerning a prophecy I had made fifteen years before, the which was failing to be fulfilled. At the end of *Sketch of my Life*, written in 1930 and available also in English, I had, with half-sportive belief in certain symmetries and numerical correspondences in my life, ventured the guess that I would pass from this world in 1945, at the age of seventy, as had my mother. The foretold year, the man said, was virtually over, and I had not kept my word. What did I want to say to the public to excuse myself for still being alive?

My reply did not please my wife at all—the less so since her anxious heart had for a considerable time been concerned about my health. She tried to stop me, to protest, to unsay the things which I was permitting an interviewer to draw from me, and which I had previously kept even from her. The fulfilment of prophecies, I said, was a curious business. Often they did not come true literally, but suggestively. Fulfilment might be a bit wide of the mark, open to question and yet unmistakable. Certain factors might be substituted for other factors. To be sure, I conceded, in spite of my desire for matters to work out in an orderly fashion, I was not yet dead. But my visitor should know that in the year I had set for it, my life had—biologically speaking—reached a low such as I had never known before. I hoped that my vital forces would help me climb out of this abyss. But my present condition seemed to me fully to bear out my prophetic gifts, and I would be glad if he and his esteemed journal would also consider it good enough.

When I spoke in these terms, three months were yet to pass before the biological low to which I had referred reached its extremity: a serious physical crisis, which forced upon me a surgical operation, for months prevented me from working, and tested my constitution in a way I had scarcely imagined possible. I mention this, however, because the experience caused me once more to note the curious divergence between biological and intellectual vitality. Periods of physical well-being and blooming health, when the body gives one no trouble at all and one's step is firm, are not at all necessarily periods of outstanding creativity. I wrote the best chapters of *Lotte in Weimar* during a six-month attack of infectious sciatica. Never have I endured such wild pain—it cannot be described to those who have not had the disease. To escape these agonizing twinges, you vainly seek the right position day and night. There is no right position. After nights which may God keep me from ever having to live again, breakfast usually brought a certain respite to my burning, inflamed nerves; and then, sitting at my desk at one strange angle or another, I would perform the *unio mystica* with Goethe, the "star of sublime beauty". Still and all, sciatica is not a disease that reaches deep into the vitals. Despite all its torture, it is not an illness to be taken very seriously. On the other hand, the time of which I am speaking, and for which I had prophesied my death, was a period of real decline in all my vital forces, of unmistakable biological "reduction". Yet this was the very period in which a work germinated, which, from the moment of its inception, has had an unusually far-reaching power.

There would be something doctrinaire about seeing a sinking of vitality as the cause and precondition for a creative effort that absorbs into itself the stuff of an entire life, that half unwittingly, half consciously synthesizes and unifies a man's entire life, and therefore embodies the vital charge which the physical self is no longer capable of. It would be easier to turn the explanation around and to blame my illness on the work. For indeed, like no other of my books, this one consumed and took heavy toll of my innermost forces. Well-meaning intimates did take the relationship in that light, and when they saw me looking so run-down were apt to comment: "It is the book." And did I not say yes? There is a noble saying: that he who gives his life shall save it—a saying as applicable to the realm of art and literature as to religion. It is never from lack of vitality that such an offering of one's life is made, and surely no such lack is shown when—strange case indeed!—at seventy a man writes his "wildest" book. Nor was there any sign of that in the agility with which I rose up from the operation, marked with a scar from chest to back, and to the amusement of the doctors rushed home to finish that book. . . .

But I want to tell the story of *Faustus*, embedded as

it is in the pressure and tumult of outward events. I want to try to reconstruct that story on the basis of my brief daily notes, for myself and for my friends.

II

In November 1942 a journey to the East delayed the completion of *Joseph the Provider*, which I had sought to bring to a conclusion during the preceding weeks, amid the thunder of the battles for burning Stalingrad. On this journey I took with me the manuscript of a lecture on the nearly finished tetralogy. The expedition led through Chicago to Washington and New York and was rich in encounters, public meetings, and appearances. Among other things, I once again saw Princeton and the friends belonging to that period of my life when I lived there: Frank Aydelotte, Einstein, Christian Gauss, Helen Lowe-Porter, Hans Rastede of the Lawrenceville School and his circle, Erich von Kahler, Hermann Broch, and others. The days in Chicago had been overshadowed by news of the war in North Africa, perturbing accounts of the march of German troops through unoccupied France, Pétain's protest, the transhipment of the Hitler Corps to Tunis, the Italian occupation of Corsica, the recapture of Tobruk. We read of feverish defensive measures by the Germans at all probable invasion points, of signs that the French fleet was preparing to go over to the side of the Allies.

The sight of Washington on a war footing was new and remarkable to me. A guest once more of Eugene Meyer and his beautiful wife in their palatial home on Crescent Place, I gazed in astonishment at the heavily militarized district around Lincoln Memorial, with its barracks, office buildings, and bridges, and at the trains laden with war materials that incessantly rolled into the city. It was oppressively hot, a belated Indian summer. At a dinner in my host's house, at which the Brazilian and Czech ambassadors were present with their wives, the discussion turned to American collaboration with Darlan and the problem of "expediency". Opinions were divided. I did not conceal my distaste for it. After dinner we heard the radio address of Wendell Willkie, who had just returned from his One-World tour. Communiqués on the important naval victory off the Solomons cheered the gathering.

To my delight, the lecture arranged at the Library of Congress brought me together once more with Archibald MacLeish, then still Librarian of Congress, and his wife. And I regarded it as a special honour that Vice-President Wallace, introduced by MacLeish, in his turn said an introductory word for me. After such a prelude, the reading itself met with a more than friendly response. My text was coloured somewhat by current events, and the loud-speaker transmitted my words to a second closely packed hall.

The evening was concluded with a reception, abounding in personalities, at the Meyers' house. There I talked chiefly with men in whom I placed much confidence, who held high positions in the Roosevelt administration: Wallace and Attorney-General Francis Biddle. The latter's pleasant wife said many kind things to me about my lecture. Biddle, with whom I had corresponded about the restrictions imposed upon "enemy aliens", particularly the German exiles, told me of his intention to remove these limitations very soon. From him I also learned that Roosevelt—whose relations with the Vichy Régime were

arousing doubts and disquiet in others beside myself—
was at any rate demanding the release of the anti-Fascists
and Jews held in North Africa.

I was grateful to our hostess, Agnes Meyer—so active
in literary, political, and social circles, and my patroness
these many years—for arranging a meeting with the
Swiss ambassador, Dr. Bruggmann, and his wife, a sister
of Henry Wallace. This conversation with the intelligent
and warm-hearted representative of the country that had
lent us its protection for five years was both pleasurable
and important to me. The subject of our talk was, of course,
the dark fate of Germany, its hopelessness now that the
possibility of capitulation seemed to be cut off. Dr. Bruggmann was convinced that the Russians would soon be pouring into Germany.

Even more important to me was the personal meeting
with Maxim Litvinov. Our hosts had invited him and his
charming British wife to lunch. The latter, extremely
sprightly, socially gifted, and quick of tongue, dominated
the conversation at table. Afterwards, however, I had the
opportunity to express to the ambassador my admiration
for his political attitudes and activity before the war, his
speeches in the League of Nations, and his insistence on
the indivisibility of peace. He had been the only one, I
said, who had consistently called things by their right
name and given truth the floor—unfortunately in vain.
He thanked me, with some melancholy. His mood seemed
to me rather morose and bitter—which was probably due
not only to the terrible trials, sacrifices, and sufferings
which the war was imposing upon his country. My impression was that his mission as mediator between East
and West was being made as hard as possible for him by
his government, and that indeed he was not likely to

remain for long at his ambassador's post in Washington.

In hours free of social obligations I tried to push forward on the current chapter of *Joseph the Provider*—already one of the last, the chapter on the blessing of the sons. But what strikes me and impresses me as something mysterious is the kind of reading that I did on this trip during train journeys, evening hours, and brief rests. Contrary to my usual habit on lecture tours, it bore no relation to my present occupation, nor to the next work I had in view. Instead, I read the memoirs of Igor Stravinsky—studied "with the pencil", that is to say, making underlinings for rereading. I also read two books long familiar to me: *Nietzsches Zusammenbruch* (*Nietzsche's Collapse*) by Erich Friedrich Podach, and Lou Andreas-Salomé's recollections of Nietzsche, which I likewise went through making pencil marks. "Fateful mysticism, unpardonable, often arousing pity. The 'unfortunate'!" That is the diary jotting apropos this reading. Music, then, and Nietzsche. I would not be able to explain why my thoughts and interests were turning in this particular direction at that time.

In our New York hotel one day the agent Armin Robinson called upon us to present, most temptingly, a plan for a book to be published not only in English but also in four or five other languages; it was to bear the title *The Ten Commandments*. The project was to have a moral and polemic slant. Ten world-famous writers were to contribute to it, each treating one of the commandments and telling the tale of some criminal breach of the moral law. They were offering me a fee of one thousand dollars for a short essay introducing the whole thing. Travelling, one is more receptive to such commissions than at home. I agreed, and two days later in the office of a lawyer—

where I met Sigrid Undset, who had likewise agreed to participate—I signed a contract full of pitfalls and barbed hooks. I had scarcely read the document, and in it I handed over to the entrepreneur the eternal rights to a work which did not yet exist, of whose development I had no conception, and which I was destined to take far more seriously than the occasion demanded. If it is foolish to buy "a pig in a poke", it is even more foolish to sell one in that manner.

The shocking war news that the commanders and crew of the French fleet had sunk their ships outside Toulon came in the midst of our days filled with going to concerts and to the theatre, with invitations and meetings with friends; days in which many bits of occasional writing had also to be dashed off. The usually quiet pages of my notebook, which I still had from Switzerland, were now sprinkled with names. The Walters and Werfels, Max Reinhardt, the actor Karlweis, Martin Gumpert, the publisher Landshoff, Fritz von Unruh figured in it; also charming old Annette Kolb, Erich von Kahler, Molly Shenstone, our British friend from Princeton, and American colleagues of the younger generation, such as Glenway Wescott, Charles Neider, and Christopher Lazare. In addition there were our children. We spent Thanksgiving Day with South American guests at Alfred Knopf's country house in Purchase.

With the German-speaking group, we had various readings from works in progress; Kahler read some extremely impressive selections from his intellectual history of the human race, which was to be published under the title of *Man the Measure*. I myself once more trotted out the grateful annunciation chapter from *Joseph the Provider*, also the cup and recognition scenes, and received the praise and encouragement which is both the reward and the aim of such readings of relatively "sure-fire" passages from the work one is struggling with. What has been carefully forged in the course of long moonings is poured out over the listeners in a rapid hour of reading; the illusion of improvisation, of polished extemporization, intensifies the impression, and when others are stirred to marvel, we for our part believe that everything is fine.

III

We returned home before the middle of December, passing on the way through San Francisco, where we visited two of the children, our youngest son, the musician, and his pretty Swiss wife, and where once more I was charmed by the sky-blue eyes of my favourite grandson, little Frido, an utterly enchanting child. I immediately resumed work on the blessing chapter. After concluding this, all I had left was to describe Jacob's death and burial, and "The Great Progress" from Egypt to Canaan. The year 1943 was only a few days old when I set down the last lines of the fourth Joseph novel and therewith brought the whole work to its end. It was a curious day for me, that fourth of January, but certainly not one marked by high spirits. This great narrative work which had accompanied me through all these years of exile, ensuring me the unity of my life, was done, was finished with, and I was unburdened—a state of doubtful weightlessness for one who since his early days, since the days of *Budden-brooks*, has lived under multifarious burdens that had to be carried long distances, and who scarcely knows how to live without them.

Antonio Borgese and his wife, our Elisabeth, were with us, and that same evening I read the two final chapters to the family circle. The impression was comforting. We drank champagne. Bruno Frank, informed of the event of the day, telephoned to congratulate me, his voice vibrant with feeling. Why I should have been "suffering, sorrowful, deeply perturbed and weary" during the next few days is something known only to God, to whose knowledge—even about Himself—we must consign so much. Perhaps the prevailing torrid winds, like a Swiss *föhn*, contributed to my state; also the news of the idiotic cruelty of the Nazis, who in spite of Swedish intervention were going to deport the eighty-three-year-old widow of Max Leibermann to Poland. She took poison instead. . . . At the same time Russian corps were advancing upon Rostov; the expulsion of the Germans from the Caucasus was nearly completed; and in a strong, confident speech to the new Congress, Roosevelt announced the invasion of Europe.

I set to work giving titles to the chapters of the fourth volume and dividing it into seven principal parts, or "books". Meanwhile I read such things as Goethe's essay, *Israel in the Desert*, Freud's *Moses*, Erich Auerbach's *Wüste und Gelobtes Land* (*Desert and Promised Land*), and also dipped into the Pentateuch. I had long been asking myself why I should contribute only an essayistic foreword to the book of stories by distinguished writers— why not rather an "organ prelude", as Werfel later put it? Why not a tale of the issuance of the Commandments, a Sinai novella? That seemed very natural to me as a postlude to the Joseph story; I was still warm from the epic.

Notes and preparations for this work required only a few days. One morning I delivered my radio broadcast on the tenth year of Nazi rule, and the next morning I began writing the Moses story. I was already in the eleventh chapter when on February 11—it happened also to be our wedding anniversary—there drew round for the tenth time the day we had left Munich with scanty baggage, without suspecting that we would not return.

In not quite two months—a short span for me, with my way of working—I wrote the story down almost without corrections. In contrast to the quasi-scientific circumstantiality of the *Joseph*, this one was swiftly paced from the start. During the writing, or perhaps even before, I had given it the title of *Das Gesetz* (*The Law*),[1] by which I was referring not only to the Decalogue but also to the moral law in general, man's civilization. It was a subject I was serious about, for all that I treated the legendary material jestingly and made use of Voltairean mockery for the characterization—again in contrast to the *Joseph* stories. Probably under the unconscious influence of Heine's portrait of Moses, I did not give my hero the features of Michelangelo's Moses but of Michelangelo himself, in order to depict him as an artist toiling laboriously over refractory human raw material and suffering dispiriting defeats. The curse at the end, against the present-day wretches to whom power was given to profane his work, the Tables of the Law, came from my heart and at least at the end leaves no doubt of the militant intent of this otherwise somewhat frivolous little thing.

The morning after completing this story I cleared away all the mythological and Oriental material that had accumulated in the course of the *Joseph*—pictures, excerpts,

---

[1] Published as *The Tables of the Law*.

17

drafts. The stuff was all packed away. The books I had read for the purpose remained on their shelves, a little library in themselves. Only one day later—March 15, to be exact—my evening notes contained the curt jotting: "Dr. Faust". This is its first mention, and only the briefest of references: "Looking through old papers for material on 'Dr. Faust'. " What papers? I can hardly say. But the notation, which occurs again the following day, is connected with letters to Professor Gustav Arlt of the University of California in Los Angeles and to MacLeish in Washington, asking for an extended loan of the Faust chapbook and—the letters of Hugo Wolf. The combination suggests that I had long been pursuing a rather definite outline of an idea which on the other hand was also extremely nebulous. Apparently the theme was to be some demonic intoxication and its liberating but catastrophic effects—the chief character to be an artist of a still unspecified sort, but evidently a complicated creature. "Going through old notes in the morning," I have down for the 27th. "Dug up the three-line outline of the Dr. Faust of 1901. Association with the Tonio Kröger period, the Munich days, the never-realized plans for *The Lovers* and *Maya*. 'Old Love, old friendship rise along with these.' Shame and strong sentimentality at remembrance of these youthful sorrows. . . ."

Forty-two years had passed since I had set down something about an artist's pact with the devil as a possible subject for a piece of writing, and the seeking and finding of these notes was accompanied by a degree of emotion, not to say inner tumult, which made one thing very clear to me: that the meagre and vague nucleus had been surrounded from the beginning by a belt of personal concern, a density of biographical feeling, which from the first

18

destined the long short story for a novel—though this was far from my mind. It was all this inner stirring which caused me to expand my usually laconic diary notes into monologues: "Only now do I realize what it means to be without the *Joseph* work, the task which always stood beside me, before me, all through this decade. Only now that *The Law* postlude is finished do I become conscious of the novelty and peril of the situation. It was comfortable, working away on what I had already dredged up. Do I still have strength for new conceptions? Have I not used up my subject matter? And if not—shall I still be able to summon up the desire for work? Gloomy weather: rainy, cold. With a headache, I drew up outline and notes for the novella. To Los Angeles for the concert; in Steinberg's box with his ladies. Horowitz played the B flat major Piano Concerto of Brahms, the orchestra did the *Don Juan* overture and Tschaikovsky's *Pathétique*. 'In compliance with many requests,' the phrase would once have been. Yet it is his melancholy best, the highest he could rise to, and there is always something beautiful and moving in seeing a limited talent reaching, by who knows what set of circumstances, the peak of its abilities. I remembered, too, how Stravinsky, years ago in Zürich, confessed to me that he admired Tschaikovsky (I had asked him about it). With the conductor in the green room. . . . Read with amusement stories in the *Gesta Romanorum*, likewise *Nietzsche und die Frauen* (*Nietzsche's Women*) by [Hellmut Walter] Brann, and Stevenson's masterpiece, *Dr. Jekyll and Mr. Hyde*, with my thoughts fixed on the Faust subject—which, however, is far from taking shape. Although the pathological aspect could be shifted into the realm of fable, could be linked with mythology, the whole thing has something forbidding about it; the difficulties seem insuperable, and it is possible that I shrink from the undertaking because I have always regarded it as my last."

Reading that over, I know that the supposition was right. Right about the lineage of the barely definable idea, whose long roots reach far down into my life—and right that in my life plan, which was always a plan of work, I had from the start kept the treatment of this idea for the end. To myself I had called this work, which might some day have to be done, my "Parsifal". Strange though it seems that a work of old age should be placed on the agenda in youth—it was so. It is likely that there is a connection between this and my conscious interest, expressed in many a critical essay, in the late works of artists—*Parsifal* itself, the second part of *Faust*, the last works of Ibsen, the prose of Adalbert Stifter and Theodor Fontane in the latter years of their lives.

The question was whether the hour had come for this task so long ago though so dimly sighted. Clearly, I felt certain instinctive scruples, reinforced by the premonition that there was something uncanny about this subject and that it would cost heart's blood, a great deal of it, to whip it into shape. Added to this was a vague notion of how radical its demands would be, how everything in it would have to be carried to extremes. This whole thing could be comprised in the cry: "Let me try something else first!" The something else, which had the merit of putting off the other project for a good long time, was to pick up and complete the fragmentary novel I had laid aside before the First World War, the *Confessions of Felix Krull, Confidence Man*.

"K." (that is my wife) "speaks of finishing the *Krull*, which friends have often petitioned for. The idea is not altogether alien to me, but I had considered the book, which springs from a period when the artist-bourgeois problem was my most dominant concern, superannuated and outmoded by the *Joseph*. Nevertheless, reading and listening to music last night, I was curiously stirred by the thought of resuming it, chiefly from the point of view of life's unity. After thirty-two years there would be something intriguing about taking up again where I left off before *Death in Venice*, for whose sake I interrupted the *Krull*. It would mean that all my major and incidental works had been an interpolation, occupying a whole generation, into the undertaking that the thirty-six-year-old had been engaged on. Also, the advantage of building on an old foundation."

What all this came to was: "Let me try something else first." And yet the thorn was in my flesh, the thorn of curiosity about the new and dangerous task. There were diversions during the next few days. I had to write some occasional pieces: a broadcast to Germany, an Open Letter to Alexei Tolstoy as a contribution to a Russian-American exchange. Then came shock at the sudden death of Heinrich Zimmer, the brilliant Indologist and husband of Christiane Hofmannsthal; I had drawn the material for *The Transposed Heads* from his great book on Indian mythology. From New York came news of a counter-movement, led by Sforza, Maritain, and others, to Coudenhove's capitalists' club—his reactionary Pan-Europe. This occupied me, made it necessary that I state my position. The War in North Africa, where Montgomery had brought Rommel to a standstill, held me in suspense. But the books I had asked for had arrived: the Faust chapbook and the collected letters of Hugo Wolf in many volumes, placed at my disposal by the Library of Congress.

And for all my sputterings on the "advantages" of resuming the *Krull*, all my diary notes of the end of March and the beginning of April reveal that I was mulling over the Faust theme.

"Extracts from the Faust chapbook. Evening, reading in it. Second air raid on Berlin in 48 hours. . . . Excerpts from Hugo Wolf's Letters. Thoughts, dreams, notes. Evening, Wolf's Letters to Grohe. The lack of judgment, the dreadful facetiousness, the enthusiasm for his bad opera libretti, the stupid remarks on Dostoevsky. Euphoric anticipations of madness which then, as in Nietzsche, expresses itself in megalomaniac ideas but has nothing of greatness about it. Sad illusions about the operas. Not a sensible word. . . . . The letters again. What form could it all take? The basic presentation is questionable. Even time and place. . . . . Notes on the Faust theme. After dinner, dipping into Paul Bekker's *Musikgeschichte* [*History of Music*], which he gave me in 1927 with the inscription 'For the train.' More reading of it when I had the chance in the evening. . . . Massive and systematic bombings of Hitler's continent. Advances of the Russians in the Crimea. Signs of imminent invasion of Europe. . . . . At Bruno and Liesl Frank's in Beverly Hills for dinner. He read his Nazi story on the Fourth Commandment. Excellently done. Some words in confidence about the plan for Faust. . . ."

What was that—was I already announcing this plan of mine to old friends, unclear though I was in my own mind concerning form, plot, manner of presentation, even time and place? How exactly had I put it? In any case, this was the first time that I opened my mouth about it, except for consultations with my wife, who favoured the new plan rather than the resumption of the old one.

Incidentally, I was not feeling well. A throat and bronchial catarrh was giving me trouble in spite of the clear, warm weather, and I found myself "very dull in spirit", unsure of myself and pessimistic about my future creativity. And yet I had only recently done things like *Tamar*, *Annunciation*, and the second half of the Moses!. . . . "Dipping into books on Nietzsche. Moved by a letter of Rohde concerning him. At night, *Murr the Tomcat* by E. T. A. Hoffmann. In Bekker's history of music, on playfulness in the art of Haydn, gaiety in the sense of being beyond jest and earnestness, the surmounting of reality."

One day, in spite of everything, I set about untying the bundles of material on the *Confidence Man* and re-reading the preliminary studies—with a result that was passing strange. It was "insight into the inner kinship of the Faust subject with this one (the motif of loneliness, in the one case mystic and tragic, in the other humorous and roguish); nevertheless my feeling is that the Faust, if I am capable of shaping it, is more appropriate for me today, more topical, more urgent. . . ." The balance had been swung. The *Joseph* business was not to be followed by a preliminary "something else" in the form of my novel about a rogue. The radically serious, menacing subject, around which the lightning of grave sacrifice seemed to flash, had proved the stronger in its demands and in its promise. Heaven grant that it would prove possible to let it partake a little of artistic playfulness and jest, irony, travesty, higher humour! My notes of the next several weeks no longer deal with anything else. I was burying myself in this new field, recollecting and summoning up material, accumulating sidelights, in order to create a body for the hovering shadow.

"On German urban life in Luther's region. Also, medical and theological reading. Gropings, attempts, and a tentative feeling of greater security in the atmosphere of the subject. Walked the mountain road with K. All day reading Luther's letters. Took up *Ulrich von Hutten* by D. F. Strauss. Decided to study books on music. Finished Bekker's history with greatest attentiveness. Nothing yet has been done about staffing the book with characters, filling it out with meaningful subsidiary figures. In *The Magic Mountain* these were provided by the personnel of the sanatorium, in *Joseph* by the Bible; there it was a question of realizing the potentialities of the Biblical figures. In *Krull* the world could permissibly have been phantasmagorical. It may be so here, too, to a certain extent; but here much full-bodied reality is needed, and for that there is a deficiency of concrete observation. . . . The characters will have to be supplied out of the past, out of memory, pictures, intuition. But the entourage must first be invented and fixed. . . ."

I wrote to Professor Paul Tillich of the Union Theological Seminary to ask about the procedures of studying for the ministry. Curiously enough, there came almost simultaneously a letter from Bermann Fischer transmitting a Swedish proposal that I write a book on Germany, its past and future. "If one could only do everything. But the demands of the era, which employs the voices of people for its purposes—at bottom we meet them, but differently from the way asked." Still and all, a letter from the Office of War Information was also received at this time, thanking me "for the article on Germany's future, which has met with much approval in Sweden". I no longer have any idea what article it referred to.

"Made extracts of Lamentation of Faust and mockery

of the 'spirit' (intended as a symphony). Notes, excerpts, meditations, and calculations on time sequence. Luther's letters. Dürer pictures. Ernest Newman's *Hugo Wolf*, in English. Thoughts on the way the subject was identified with things German, with German solitude in the world in general. Symbolic values here . . . Reading of the *Witches' Hammer*. Details of youth in Munich. Figure of Rud. Schwerdtfeger, violinist in the Zapfenstösser orchestra (!) . . . Drawing up a list of characters for the novel, and their names. *Pascal and the Medieval Definition of God* by Nitze. . . ."

Amid such surveys and studies the month of May 1943 began, a month in which the tenderest, most delicate impressions and feelings were coupled with a striving, testing, inventing which had already become the dominant factor in my life and which arrogated for its own purposes all that reality brought my way. The children from San Francisco came for a longish visit, "with the two boys, who look fine and strong. Moved, as always, by Frido's beautiful eyes. Went walking with him before dinner. He ate with us. . . . . Much jesting with the little fellow, who is just beginning to talk." Tuesday, May 4: "In the afternoon, on the promenade with little Fridolin. When the walk is over, he says 'Nuff'. This for Nepomuk Schneidewein. Evening, reading the *Malleus Maleficarum*. . . . Frido is very attached to me. . . . After the walk, lunch with him in the Miramar; the child was very well behaved."

A letter to Bruno Walter in New York was written about this time, "not without connection with the subject" —that is to say, with the sketch of the novel, and incidentally full of stories and anecdotes about the charming child. In reply, Walter expressed warm interest in the plan for a "musician novel", saying that few were so called to it as I. He also made what I referred to—I know not with what feelings—as "a remarkable suggestion"; namely, that Frido should play a part in the book—he could imagine the episode, he said, as an *allegretto moderato*. This dear friend and splendid musician had no notion of the cold breath of inhumanity that blows through the book at the end. He could not know that I would be constrained to tell the story of the child of God in quite another spirit from that of *allegretto moderato*.

A sizeable pile of notes had accumulated, testifying to the complexity of the plan. I found I had some two hundred half-quarto sheets: a wild medley of disordered, boxed-in notes from many fields—linguistic, geographic, politico-social, theological, medical, biological, historical, and musical. I was still continuing to gather and hoard everything useful to my purpose, but I find it good to see that, in spite of such preoccupation and obsession, my mind was still open to impressions from outside the magic circle, from the world that did not pertain to the novel. "Read an excellent article in the *Nation*, a piece by Henry James on Dickens," I set down one day. "Written in 1864 at the age of twenty-two. Amazing! Is there anything like it in Germany? The critical writings of the West are far superior. . . . Extensive reading in Niebuhr's book, *The Nature and Destiny of Man* . . . Till after midnight reading in its entirety Stifter's wonderful *Rock Crystal*." But then, too: "The coal miner strike, serious crisis. Government takeover of the mines. Troops to protect those willing to work—which will be few. . . . Read some curious things on the inglorious defeat of the Germans in Africa. Nothing of Nazi fanaticism's 'to the last drop of blood. . . .' Talking in the evening with Bruno

Frank about the new strike wave here and the administration's responsibility for it. Concern about the American home front . . . Heaviest bombing of Dortmund, with more than a thousand planes. All Europe in invasion fever. Preparations of the French underground organization. Announcement of general strike. The garrison in Norway is instructed to fight 'to the last man'—which never happens. In Africa 200,000 prisoners were taken. Superiority of matériel in quantity and quality explains the victory. . . . Expectation of the invasion of Italy. Undertakings against Sardinia and Sicily are in the offing. . . . In the evening read *Love's Labour's Lost.*"

The Shakespeare play is pertinent. It falls within the magic circle—while around it sounds the uproar of the world. "Supper with the Werfels and Franks. Conversation on Nietzsche and the pity he arouses—for his and for more general desperation. Meetings with Schönberg and Stravinsky planned. . . . Calculations of time and age relationships in the novel, vital statistics and names. . . . On Riemenschneider and his time. Purchases. Volbach's *Instrumentenkunde* [a handbook of musical instruments]. Notes concerning Leverkühn as musician. His given name to be Anselm, Andreas, or Adrian. Notes on Fascist ideology of the period. Gathering at the Werfels with the Schönbergs. Pumped S. a great deal on music and the life of a composer. To my deep pleasure, he himself insists we must all get together more often. . . . The Alfred Neumanns with us for supper. While the ladies were preparing the meal (we are without a maid), I expound the plan of the novel to N., who was stirred to amazement."

I shall never forget that. This faithful friend, for whom I had always had such high regard, listened with exclamations of the keenest interest. His attitude confirmed me in all I had felt about the book—all the pleasure and pain which emanated from the idea as I outlined it to him, my words coming to me swiftly and easily. What most impressed him, I think, was the central idea: the flight from the difficulties of the cultural crisis into the pact with the devil, the craving of a proud mind, threatened by sterility, for an unblocking of inhibitions at any cost, and the parallel between pernicious euphoria ending in collapse with the nationalistic frenzy of Fascism. I heard later that on the drive home he spoke to his wife the whole way of what I had confided to him.

On May 23, 1943, a Sunday morning little more than two months after I had fetched out that old notebook, and also the date on which I had my narrator, Serenus Zeitblom, set to work, I began writing *Doctor Faustus*.

IV

My diary of the period does not record exactly when I made the decision to interpose the medium of the "friend" between myself and my subject; in other words, not to tell the life of Adrian Leverkühn directly but to have it told, and therefore not to write a novel but a biography with all its trappings. Assuredly, recollection of the sham autobiography of Felix Krull influenced me here. Besides, this strategy was a bitter necessity in order to achieve a certain humorous leavening of the sombre material and to make its horrors bearable to myself as well as to the reader. To make the demonic strain pass through an undemonic medium, to entrust a harmless and simple soul, well-meaning and timid, with the recital of the story, was in itself a comic idea. It removed some of the burden, for it enabled me to escape the turbulence of everything direct, personal, and confessional which underlay the baneful conception, to steer it into indirection and to travesty it as I depicted it through the eyes of this good, unheroic soul, who could only wring his hands and shake his head at these events.

But above all, the interposition of the narrator made it possible to tell the story on a dual plane of time, to weave together the events which shake the writer as he writes with those he is recounting, so that the quivering of his hand is ambiguously and yet obviously explained both by the vibration of distant bomb hits and by his inner consternation.

That Professor Zeitblom begins his narrative on the same day that I myself put the first lines on paper is characteristic of the entire book, of the curious brand of reality that clings to it, which seen from one aspect is total artifice. It is part of the playful effort to achieve precise— precise to the point of being infuriating—realization of something fictional: the biography and the character of Leverkühn. This work, moreover, took a curiously ruthless form, and I was constantly amazed by the way its fantastic mechanisms drew upon factual, historical, personal, and even literary data. As in the "panoramas" shown in my childhood, palpable reality was for ever indistinguishably merging into painted perspectives and illusions. This montage technique was continually startling, even to me, and gave me cause to worry. Yet it rightly belongs to the conception, to the "idea", of the book; it has to do with the strange and licentious spiritual relaxation from which it emerged, with its figurative and then again literal directness, its character as arcanum and confession, so that, as long as I was working on the book, the concept of its public existence did not enter my mind.

The smuggling of living persons, named flatly by name, among the characters of the novel, with whom they take their place, equally real or unreal, is only a minor example of the montage principle I am speaking of. There is the interweaving of Leverkühn's tragedy with that of Nietzsche, whose name does not appear in the entire book—advisedly, because the euphoric musician has been made so much Nietzsche's substitute that the original is no longer permitted a separate existence. There is the taking of Nietzsches's experience in the Cologne bordello and of the symptomatology of his disease; there are the devil's quotations from *Ecce Homo;* also the borrowings from diet menus to be found in Nietzsche's letters from Nice (which must have escaped the attention of most readers). I likewise borrowed from Paul Deussen's account of his last visit to his deranged friend, to whom he brought a bouquet of flowers. Quotations of this kind have something musical about them, disregarding the innate mechanical quality. They are, moreover, reality transformed into fiction, fiction that absorbs the real, and thus a strangely protean and attractive mingling of the spheres. I also quoted—but this is obvious—from the biography of Tschaikovsky, whose invisible friend, Frau von Meck, is here presented as Madame de Tolna. The story of the wooing is also quoted from reality, the reckless—though it was in truth by no means reckless—putting of a proposal through a friend.

Since there is so much Nietzsche in the novel that it has been called a Nietzsche novel, it becomes easy to assume that the triangle of Adrian, Marie Godeau, and Rudi Schwerdtfeger is a straight picture of Nietzsche's pro-

posals to Lou Andreas through Rée, and to Fräulein
Trampedach through Hugo von Senger (who was already
half engaged to her). But, even seen from the point of
view of Leverkühn himself, the triangle is rather a
Shakespearean reminiscence, a quotation from the sonnets, which Adrian always has by him and whose plot—
the relationship of poet, lover, and friend; the motif of the
treacherous wooing, that is—is also a theme of several
of the plays. These very plays, in fact, lie upon the musician's desk: *Twelfth Night, Much Ado about Nothing*, and
Two Gentlemen of Verona. And Adrian takes mischievous
delight in weaving into his remarks to Zeitblom, who is
no more aware of it than the reader, direct quotations
from these plays. His curiously formal phrase, "You
would be obliging me very much by this friendly service,"[1]
is a quote from *Much Ado about Nothing*, where Claudio
confesses to the prince his love for Hero. Later he repeats
the bitter "Friends are like that today,"[2] from *Two
Gentlemen of Verona*, and cites almost word for word the
verses:

> Whom can you trust, when your own right hand
> Strikes you in the breast?[3]

In the persuasion scene between himself and Rudi in
Pfeiffering, one of my favourite scenes in the book, he
justifies his fatal request with these words from *Twelfth
Night*:

[1] This and the following quotations from Shakespeare have undergone
some irreversible changes in the transmutations from English into German
and from German back into English. Apparently Thomas Mann did not
inform the translator of *Doctor Faustus* of the hidden quotations in the
German text. In the text of *Much Ado about Nothing* the original line
reads: "My liege, your highness now may do me good."
[2] Shakespeare's original: "For such a friend is now."
[3] Original: "Who should be trusted, when one's own right hand
Is perjur'd to the bosom."

31

> She will incline her ear to your words more than to anything
> Such a sobersides would say.[4]

And afterwards, purportedly lamenting his folly, he once again quotes from *Much Ado about Nothing*, citing to Zeitblom the image of the foolish schoolboy "who finds a bird's nest and out of sheer joy shows it to another boy, who then goes and steals it".[5] Whereupon Serenus, to top it off, unconsciously joins in the game of quotation as he replies: "It is no sin or shame to be trusting, surely; they are the portion of the thief".[6] He comes perilously close to saying, literally: "The transgression is in the stealer."

It was Frank Harris who in his ingenious book on Shakespeare pointed out that the wooing motif of the sonnets recurs three times in the plays. In *Faustus* it takes a peculiar form of montage. Adrian, governed by his special relationship with the "wooer" Schwerdtfeger, deliberately and with sinister playfulness repeats a cliché, or myth, with dread purpose. On the devil's instigation, with malice aforethought, he is bringing Rudi to his death—and Zeitblom knows it.

Ought I also to cite as an example of such an act of montage and theft from reality an element which many persons have found objectionable; namely, Adrian Leverkühn's appropriation of Schönberg's concept of the twelve-tone or row system of music? I suppose I must, and from now on the book, at Schönberg's request, is to carry a postscript spelling out the intellectual property rights for

[4] Original: "She will attend it better in thy youth
Than in a nuncio of more grave aspect."
[5] Original: "Who being overjoyed with finding a bird's nest, shows it to his companion and he steals it."
[6] Original: "Wilt thou make a trust a transgression?"

the uninformed. This is being done a bit against my own convictions—not so much because such an explanation knocks a small rounded breach into the rounded, integral world of my novel, as because, within the sphere of the book, within this world of a pact with the devil and of black magic, the idea of the twelve-tone technique assumes a colouration and a character which it does not possess in its own right and which—is this not so?—in a sense make it really my property, or, rather, the property of the book. Schönberg's idea and my *ad hoc* version of it differs so widely that, aside from the stylistic fault, it would have seemed almost insulting, to my mind, to have mentioned his name in the text.

V

When I began to write, that Sunday morning, my notes were scanty and there was no actual written outline. Yet the book, in so far as the sequence of events was concerned, must have lain plainly before my eyes; I must have had a fairly good over-all view of it to be able at once to take up its entire complex of motifs, to give the beginning the perspective in depth of the whole, and to play the part of the tremulous biographer so filled with his subject that he is always haplessly anticipating and losing himself in later developments. His nervousness was mine; I was parodying my own overbrimming eagerness. And it was a boon to play this part; to let the book be written for me, as it were; to be conscious of the indirectness of my responsibility along with such intense resolve to achieve directness; to fling into the game reality and my private world. How necessary the mask and the playfulness were, in view of the earnestness of my task—and this I was clearly conscious of from the very start. If earlier works of mine had assumed a monumental character, at least in size, they had done so unexpectedly and unintentionally. *Buddenbrooks*, *The Magic Mountain*, the *Joseph* stories, even *Lotte in Weimar* had been intended originally as extremely modest little narratives, and had grown. Only *Buddenbrooks*, in fact, had been conceived as a novel, and *Lotte in Weimar* as at best a small one—the words *A Small Novel* stand on the title page of the manuscript. This time, however, in this work of my old age, it was different. This one time I knew what I was setting out to do and what task I was imposing upon myself: to write nothing less than the novel of my era, disguised as the story of an artist's life, a terribly imperilled and sinful artist. For all my curiosity and eagerness, I was not at ease about the business. To propose that a work be big in every sense, to plan it so from the start, was probably not right—neither for the work nor for the state of mind of the author. Therefore I must introduce as much jesting, as much ridicule of the biographer, as much anti-self-important mockery as possible—as much of all that as was humanly possible. And the wife of my narrating humanist was to be named Helene Ölhafen.

The very day after I had begun, I again had an occasional piece to write to meet the demands of the hour: one of my monthly broadcasts in German, this one to commemorate the book burnings. By the end of May, the manuscript of the book consisted of no more than two pages. June was broken in the middle by a lecture trip to San Francisco, which, aside from the literary preparation for it, cost me more days than I liked. Nevertheless, in the course of that month, during which I had my sixty-eighth birthday, four chapters of *Faustus* were written. And on June 28, according to my diary, came the first reading from the novel. "The Franks for supper. Later, in my study, read aloud from *Doctor Faust*, the first three chapters. Was deeply moved, and the hearers proved receptive to the aura of excitement that emanated from it all."

Strauss's biography of Ulrich von Hutten occupied me. Professor Tillich replied to my questions about studying for the ministry. I read Luther's commentary on the *Apocalypse* and Berlioz' memoirs in English translation. At an evening gathering at Feuchtwanger's we met Miss Dodd, daughter of the former American ambassador to Hitler's Germany, the actor Homolka, and among others Franz Werfel, who took occasion to tell me about his new novel project, the utopian fantasy *Star of the Unborn*, and of the enormous difficulties it involved. Here was a comrade —one who had also let himself in for something insane, probably impossible. . . .

A few days later Ernst Křenek's book, *Music Here and Now*, came my way. It proved to be a remarkably useful work of reference. "Much reading of Křenek's *Music*" recurs several times in the diary. At the same time I stumbled across some curious information, in some magazine, concerning spiritual music among the Seventh-Day Baptists of Pennsylvania, with emphasis on the strange figure of Johann Conrad Beissel, whom I then and there decided to include in the lectures with which Kretschmar the Stammerer opens up the world of music to young Adrian (and to the reader)—the buffoon "systematician" and schoolmaster whose memory haunts the whole novel.

It was almost alarming to see what concern the technical

musical aspect of the book was giving me. For one of the chief demands of the book was a command of these technicalities, at least to the extent that no professional (and there is no more jealously guarded profession) could laugh at me. After all, I had always been very close to music, had drawn infinite stimulation and many artistic lessons from it, had as a storyteller made use of its practices and as a critical essayist described its products—so much so that a prominent member of the guild, Ernst Toch, had defined my "music making" as "abolishing the boundary between music as specialty and as a universal element". The trouble was that this time the "universal element" did not suffice, that it was practically the same as blundering amateurishness. The "specialty" was needed. There is nothing sillier, in a novel about an artist, than merely to assert the existence of art, to talk about genius, about works, to hail these and rave about their effects upon the souls of their audiences. No, concrete reality, exactitude, were needed—this was utterly clear to me. "I shall have to study music," I said to my brother when I told him of my project. And at the same time my diary confesses: "Technical musical studies frighten and bore me." That does not mean that I lacked the urge and industry to penetrate, by reading and research, into the realm of musical technique, life and creativity, just as I had, in the interest of the *Joseph*, for example, penetrated into the world of Orientalism, primitive religion, and myth. I could list a small catalogue of books on music and musicians in English and German, certainly a good two dozen, which I studied "with the pencil", reading with that earnestness and alertness that one employs only for creative ends, for the sake of a work in progress. But all this peripheral contact was not actual study of music; it would not save me from exposing my ignorance in exact details; and it did not equip me to build up the lifework of an important composer so that it really seemed as if the compositions could be heard, so that they were absolutely believable (and this is what I demanded of myself). To do that I needed outside aid, an adviser, an expert in the subject who was also capable of great insight into my literary intentions, who could serve as the knowledgeable instructor sharing my imaginative efforts. Such help would be all the more welcome since the music, in so far as the novel treats of it (for, to be sure, the novel also practises it—but that is a subject in itself)—the music was only foreground and representation, only a paradigm for something more general, only a means to express the situation of art in general, of culture, even of man and the intellect itself in our so critical era. A novel of music? Yes. But it was also conceived as a novel of the culture and the era. It was therefore of supreme importance to achieve precise realization of the means and the foreground, and that I should accept help with this was something that I regarded as utterly self-evident and natural.

The helper, adviser, and sympathetic instructor was found—one who, through exceptional technical knowledge and intellectual attainments, was precisely the right person. "Book, *Eingebung im musikalischen Schaffen* [*Inspiration in Musical Creation*]," is recorded for an early date in July 1943. "Important. Brought by Dr. Adorno". As a matter of fact, the book in question turned out to have no special importance for my work. But the name of the bringer (who must have known what I was engaged in) bobs up again some two weeks later—it was the time of the taking of Palermo and of the great Russian offensive, and I was in the midst of the seventh chapter of *Faustus*.

"Manuscript from Dr. Adorno, *Zur Philosophie der modernen Musik* [*On the Philosophy of Modern Music*]. . . . Reading Adorno's book. . . . Studying Adorno's manuscript. . . . In the evening, more reading of the manuscript, which is very instructive and at the same time points up the vast difficulty of my project. . . . Finished reading Adorno's essay. Moments of illumination on Adrian's position. The difficulties must reach their highest peak before they can be overcome. The desperate situation of art: the most vital factor. Must not lose sight of the main idea of ill-gotten inspiration, whose ecstasy carries it beyond itself. . . ."

Here indeed was something important. The manuscript dealt with modern music both on an artistic and on a sociological plane. The spirit of it was remarkably forward-looking, subtle and deep, and the whole thing had the strangest affinity to the idea of my book, to the "composition" in which I lived and moved and had my being. The decision was made of itself: this was my man.

Theodor Wiesengrund-Adorno was born in 1903 in Frankfurt-am-Main. His father was a German Jew; his mother, herself a singer, was the daughter of a French army officer of Corsican—originally Genoese—descent and of a German singer. He is a cousin of Walter Benjamin, harried to death by the Nazis, who left behind an amazingly perspicacious and profound book on German tragedy (*Deutsches Trauerspiel*) which is actually a philosophy and history of allegory. Adorno—he has taken his mother's maiden name—is a person of similar mental cast, uncompromising, tragically brilliant, operating on the highest level. Having grown up in an atmosphere entirely dominated by theory (political theory as well) and artistic, primarily musical, interests, he studied philosophy and music. In 1931 he assumed the post of lecturer at Frankfurt University and taught philosophy there until he was expelled by the Nazis. Since 1941 he has been living in Los Angeles, so close to us as to be almost a neighbour.

All his life this man of remarkable intellect has refused to choose between the professions of philosophy and music. He felt that he was actually pursuing the same thing in both divergent realms. His dialectic turn of mind and bent toward social history is interlinked with a passion for music; the phenomenon is no longer unique nowadays and is doubtless connected with the whole complex of problems of our time. In pursuit of this passion, he studied composition and piano, at first with music instructors in Frankfurt, then with Alban Berg and Eduard Steuermann in Vienna. From 1928 to 1931 he was editor of the Vienna *Anbruch*, and was active in promoting radical modern music.

But then how is it that this radicalism, which the layman tends to think of as a kind of musical sans-culottism, is accompanied by an intense feeling for tradition, a distinctly historical attitude, and an unswerving insistence upon technical mastery and craft discipline—such as I have found time and again among musicians of this type? What they deplore in Wagner is not so much his romanticism, his excess, his bourgeois character, or his demagoguery. Rather, it is very simply that he so often "composes badly". I cannot judge Adorno's compositions. But his knowledge of tradition, his mastery of the whole historical body of music, is enormous. An American singer who works with him said to me: "It is incredible. He knows every note in the world."

The manuscript he brought me at the time, whose startling pertinency to the world of my novel instantly arrested me, dealt largely with Schönberg, his school, and the twelve-tone technique. The author professes his belief in Schönberg's commanding importance, but then goes on to subject the system to a profound and searching criticism. In a pithy, excessively sharpened style that owes much to Nietzsche and still more to Karl Kraus,[1] he shows the dire consequences that must flow from the constructive Schönbergian approach to music. However necessary it may objectively be to subject music to rigorous rational analysis, and however illuminating that may be, the effect is just the converse of rationality. Over the head of the artist, as it were, the art is cast back into a dark, mythological realm. What could fit better into my world of the "magic square"? I discovered in myself, or, rather, rediscovered as a long familiar element in myself, a mental alacrity for appropriating what I felt to be my own, what belonged to me, that is to say, to the "subject". The analysis of the row system and the criticism of it that is translated into dialogue in Chapter XXII of *Faustus* is entirely based upon Adorno's essay. So are certain remarks on the tonal language of the later Beethoven, such as occur early in the book in Kretschmar's sputterings: the comments on the uncanny relationship that death establishes between genius and convention. These ideas, too, I had encountered in Adorno's manuscript, with a feeling of their strange familiarity. As for the—what word shall I use?—serenity with which I put my version of them into the mouth of my stammerer, I have only this to say: after prolonged activity of the mind it frequently happens that things which we once upon a time threw upon the waters return to us recast by another's hand and put into different

---

[1] Viennese satirist, critic, and poet (1874-1936), founder and editor of the polemical review *Die Fackel*.

relationships but still reminding us of what was once our own. Ideas about death and form, the self and the objective world, may well be regarded by the author of a Venetian novel of some thirty-five years ago as recollections of himself. They could well have their place in the younger man's musicological essay and at the same time serve me in my canvas of persons and an epoch. An idea as such will never possess much personal and proprietary value in the eyes of an artist. The thing that matters is the way it functions within the framework of his creation.

Towards the end of September 1943, though I was already working on Chapter IX, I was by no means satisfied with the existing version of Chapter VIII, Kretschmar's lectures. One evening after dinner at our house I read Chapter VIII to Adorno. "At table talking about fine points of musical philosophy. Afterwards, reading of the lecture chapter. Intimacy with music gloriously confirmed. Questions about certain details, some of which are easily amended, some not so easily. On the whole reassured."

That reassurance did not last. The next several days were again devoted to corrections, refinements, additions to the lecture chapter. Early in October (I had meanwhile again proceeded with Chapter IX), we spent an evening at the Adornos'. Our mood was grave. Franz Werfel had just had his first severe heart attack and seemed to be recovering slowly and painfully. I read three pages concerning the piano which I had recently interpolated into my alarmingly hypertrophic chapter, and our host read to us from his studies and aphorisms on Beethoven—in which a certain quotation from Musaeus' *Rübezahl* played a part. The ensuing conversation passed from humanity as the purified chthonian element to parallels between

Beethoven and Goethe, to humaneness as romantic re-sistance to society and convention (Rousseau) and as rebellion (the prose scene in Goethe's *Faust*). Then Adorno sat down at the piano and, while I stood by and watched, played for me the entire Sonata Opus 111 in a highly in-structive fashion. I had never been more attentive. I rose early the following morning and for the next three days immersed myself in a thorough-going revision and exten-sion of the lecture on the sonata, which became a significant enrichment and embellishment of the chapter and indeed of the whole book. Into the poetic little illustrative phrases I wrote for the arietta theme I slipped Adorno's patron-ymic, *Wiesengrund* (*Meadowland*), by way of showing my gratitude.

Months later—it was by then early 1944—on the oc-casion of a gathering at our house, I read to him and Max Horkheimer, his friend and colleague of the Institute for Social Research, the first three chapters of the novel, and then the Opus 111 episode. The reading made an extra-ordinary impression—intensified, it seemed, by the contrast between the strongly German basis and colour-ation of the book and my own altogether disparate private attitude towards the maniacal country of our origin. Adorno, fascinated by the musical material and, moreover, touched by the little tribute to him, came up to me and said: "I could listen all night!"

I kept him close by me henceforth, knowing that I would have need of his aid, of his above all, in the remoter reaches of the novel.

VI

On July 24, 1943, we celebrated my wife's sixtieth birthday. Many a pensive recollection came to mind of the first period of our exile, in Sanary-sur-Mer, where we had celebrated her fiftieth, of the since deceased friend who had been with us then, René Schickele. Among the congratulatory telegrams was one from our Erika, now a war correspondent in Cairo. The news of Mussolini's fall came about this time ; Badoglio had been appointed premier and commander in chief, and further liquidations would certainly follow, in spite of official assurance that "we shall keep our pledges and continue the war". The army had already taken over the militia; demonstrations were breaking out all over the country, hailing the end of Mussolini and calling for peace; and newspapers shifted their line radically. *"Siamo liberi!"* was the cry of the *Corriere della Sera.*

I was absorbed in Anton Schindler's biography of Beethoven, an intellectually limited, philistine book, but full of interesting anecdotes and useful facts. The Kretzschmar chapter was well along, but my diary notes of those days speak of fatigue and depression, of my decision to put the novel aside now, for I had been forcing its pace, and work instead on a lecture I had promised to give in Washington in the fall. I hoped that in this interval my enthusiasm for the "devil's book" would be refreshed. "After seventy pages the story initial impetus is exhausted. I must make a break, but I do not feel myself fit for anything else either". However, a task came my way which I had no trouble fulfilling, something for a fellow-writer, and one dear to me. The exiles were planning a celebration

43

for Alfred Döblin's sixty-fifth birthday. Berthold Viertel was getting together an album of handwritten congratulations, and I covered a handsome folio sheet of parchment with the words of deeply felt veneration for the powerful talent of the author of *Berlin Alexanderplatz* and *Wallenstein*, who was leading a life of altogether unmerited obscurity in America. I attended the celebration itself, in the Playhouse on Montana Avenue. There was a fine programme of recitations and music. My brother Heinrich spoke, and in conclusion the chief figure himself made a well-turned, sympathetic speech. "Over the punch afterwards," my diary records, "conversation with Döblin and Ernst Toch on the latter's music. His surprising admiration for Pfitzner's *Palestrina*. 'Too much fuss is made about atonality,' he said. 'It is unimportant.' The eternally romantic quality of music. . . ."

Notes on the lecture and its organization occupied me. This is the lecture that later appeared in the *Atlantic Monthly* under the title of "What is German". I dictated the first draft to my wife, amplified it by hand, finished the dictation, and after an interruption of two weeks once again went back to the novel, making corrections and moving ahead. I read aloud several earlier chapters, with Bruno and Liesl Frank as receptive listeners, with the idea of spurring myself onward. "Disturbing effect— which is the right, the innate effect of the book." Outward circumstances were also disturbing, however—the political undercurrents of the war, a subject which in talk with friends took precedence over personal difficulties. "Talking with our friends of the poor relationship to Russia, the disunity, the distrust nourished by the absence of a real second front; the recall of Litvinov and Maisky. Impression that what is going on is scarcely concerned with

this war any longer, but with the preparation of the next."
That was written in August 1943. . . .

The magnetism of a concern that fills the whole soul
is powerful and mysterious. Among people it will, without
the conscious intention of the person concerned, guide the
conversation, draw it irresistibly into its sphere of attraction. It governs, forms, and colours external experiences,
social encounters. The social occasions that at that time
interrupted the even tenor of my life had, as if by hazard,
a musical cast. "Dining with the Schönbergs in Brentwood.
Excellent Viennese coffee. Talking with Sch. at length
about music. . . ." "Soirée at the Werfels' with Stravinsky;
talked about Schönberg. . . ." "Buffet dinner at Schönbergs'
to celebrate his sixty-ninth birthday. Many guests. Talked
with Gustav Arlt, Klemperer, Frau Heims-Reinhardt.
Spent some time with Klemperer and Schönberg. Talked
too much. . . ."

At this time Schönberg sent me his book on harmony,
the *Harmonielehre*, and the libretto of his oratorio, *Jacob's
Ladder*, whose religious poetry I found impure. On the
other hand, I was all the more impressed by his extraordinary textbook, whose pedagogic attitude is one of
sham conservatism, the strangest mingling of piety towards tradition and revolution.

At this period, too, we began to see much of Artur
Rubinstein and his family. There is something absolutely
rejuvenating for me in observing the life of this fortunate
virtuoso. Courted and hailed for his enormous talent,
which overleaps all difficulties; possessed of a flourishing
household, marvellous health, all the money he wants;
taking intellectual and sensuous pleasure in his collections,
his precious books and paintings—everything conspires
to make him one of the happiest persons I have ever met.

He has command of six languages—if not more. His cosmopolitan, merry conversation, along with his knack of giving the drollest imitations of people, makes him shine in salons as he shines on the platform. His tremendous artistry makes him a success in every part of the globe. He does not deny his good fortune and certainly is conscious of what it means. I have noted down as characteristic of him the instinctive mutual respect for "the other art" which came out in a few words we once had. He and his wife, along with the Stravinskys and a few other guests, had spent an evening with us, and I said to him in parting: "Dear Mr. Rubinstein, you must know how greatly honoured I feel to have had you here with us." He burst into laughter. "You do? Now that will be one of my funny stories!"

The work on the chapter of the four lectures wore on deep into September, the month of the capture of Sorrento, Capri, and Ischia, the German evacuation of Sardinia and the retreat towards the Dnieper line in Russia, the preparations for the Moscow conference. Our minds were much occupied with speculation on the future of Germany, for which the Russians obviously had one plan and the West another. But the habit of isolating the first hours of the day altogether from the pressure of events, and of recognizing only one concern during these hours, helped me to concentrate. "Ardently at work on Chapter VIII. New mood of work for these strange and extremely personal labours. . . . I am going ahead and boldly writing Kretschmar's lectures out in full, with the certainty that they will be able to stand as they are. . . . Worked eagerly on the chapter (Beethoven). Did still more on the novel in the afternoon (difficult). . . ."

The literary event of these days was a public reading by

Bruno Frank, at which a large part of the German colony was present. It made me wonder. "Talented and fine, as always; moreover, excellently read. But what strikes me as odd is this: he uses the humanistic narrative style of Zeitblom with complete seriousness as his own. In matters of style I really no longer admit anything but parody. In this, close to Joyce. . . ."

I was reading the memoirs of Hector Berlioz. "His mockery of Palestrina. His contempt for the Italian temper in music and, incidentally, for the French vein as well. The Italians' lack of feeling for instrumental music (Verdi). He also questions their sense of harmony. Mere 'song-birds'. He himself, with his incessant naïve boasting, reminds me strikingly of Benvenuto Cellini."

The overbrimming lecture chapter was provisionally completed during the first twenty days of September, in infernal heat, and I began on the nineteenth, in which Adrian's musical education is carried forward. In this chapter his description of the Leonore Overture No. 3 gave me the most pleasure. I recall an evening with Leonhard Frank, who was working on his delicate novel of a woman's life, *Mathilde*, from which he read aloud to us. To my surprise he spoke at table of how stirred he had been by what he had heard of *Doctor Faustus*. He was sure, he said, that he would like this book more than any of my others; it touched at the roots of his nature. I understood very well what he meant. Socialist in his political beliefs and an admirer of Russia, he was at the same time filled with a new feeling for Germany and its indivisibility. Given the tenacity with which Hitler's troops were still fighting, this was a patriotism that seemed curiously premature. Yet it was beginning to develop among the

German exiles and was to be given highly poetic expression a little later in Frank's *Deutsche Novelle* (*A German Story*). His emotional involvement with *Faustus* was welcome to me but at the same time worried me. I could not help taking it as a warning—against the danger of my novel's doing its part in creating a new German myth, flattering the Germans with their "demonism". I saw my colleague's praise, therefore, as behoving me to proceed with caution. The themes of the book, crisis themes, had an extremely German colouration; I must attempt, as much as possible, to fuse them in the universalities of the era and of Europe. And yet I could not keep from including the word *German* in the sub-title. At the time of which I am speaking this sub-title had a provisional and rather inappropriate form: *The strange life of Adrian Leverkühn, as told by a friend*. A year later the colourless *strange life* was out, and I had instead *The Life of the German Composer*.

There were always the demands of the day intervening upon my main task. Now I would have to write a new radio broadcast for Germany, now a lecture for the Jewish women's organization, Hadassah, or a speech for a meeting of Writers in Exile held early in October, before a large audience, in the Education Building on the Westwood campus. An Englishwoman presided. Lion Feuchtwanger spoke, also a Frenchman named Périgord, a Greek by the name of Minotis, Professor Gustav Arlt and myself. Once more I found that public activity, a visit to the world of humanity, for the likes of me is prone to take on a character of fantasy, dream, and buffoonery, so that when I describe such an affair in my books I am not adding this element for literary effect; rather, that is just how these affairs appear to me. Minotis' wife was in bed at home, suffering from peritonitis. The man himself was very pale and wore mourning, as if his wife were already dead. (I have no idea whether she died.) This was the chief impression I carried home from the meeting.

One of the widest gaps in the writing of *Faustus* was caused by a journey to the East and to Canada, to which I had committed myself some time before. Begun on October 9, it was a trip marked by many stops, and it held up my work for a full two months. However, I did not part with the manuscript; the as yet meagre pages came along with me in a brief-case which also contained my lecture notes and which I never left in the care of a porter. No sooner had I reached Chicago, on my way through to the East, than I received via my brother-in-law, the physicist Peter Pringsheim, a highly significant gift from a colleague of his at the university. It was nothing less than the apparatus for making "osmotic growths" of the kind Father Leverkühn dabbles in at the beginning of the novel: a vessel containing a solution of water-glass and the necessary crystals for "sowing". I carried this curious gift with me for weeks, to Washington, New York, Boston, and Montreal. And one evening in our New York hotel, after a supper at Voisin's, with many a mock shudder, we had a crack at the pseudobiological experiment. By we I mean ourselves and a group of our friends, among them dear Annette Kolb, Martin Gumpert, Fritz Landshoff, and our Erika. I had just read aloud the first chapters of *Doctor Faustus*, and now we actually watched the muddy water sprouting those coloured shoots which Jonathan Leverkühn had found so melancholy, while Adrian had been moved to laughter.

In Washington we stayed, as always, with our oldest American friends and patrons, Eugene and Agnes Meyer, in their handsome house on Crescent Place, a centre of the city's social life. The news of Italy's coming over to the side of the Allies, her declaration of war against Germany, reached us there. Once again I spoke at the Library of Congress, introduced by MacLeish, and two days later I talked at Hunter College in New York. That same evening we went on to Boston. There it was Gaetano Salvemini, whom I was overjoyed to see again, who introduced me to the public in a most engaging address. The audience was large. Hundreds had to be turned away, and the utterly quiet attentiveness of those who listened to my one and a quarter hour's reading had, as always, something overwhelming about it for me. "What brings these people to hear me?" I ask myself. "Am I Caruso? What do they expect? And do they find their expectations in the slightest fulfilled?"

It would seem so. But of course the strangest misplacements and misunderstandings also occur, for, as a stop-gap, agents will sometimes sell one to a place where one has no business to be and cuts the oddest figure. That is how it was in a small industrial town where some sort of provincial public meeting was being held in the good cause of collecting money for aid to the war-torn countries. The whole affair took place with doors open, amid the coming and going of the crowd, with plenty of band music, rousing speeches, and popular jokes. My lecture, completely out of place as it was, was evidently the wind-up of the variegated programme. At short notice I cut it down to half an hour in manuscript, and in speaking condensed it to twenty minutes. But this was still far too long, and, above all, not a word was suitable. All the while I spoke, people were pouring out of the hall "to catch their buses and trains". At the end the chairman assured me that the whole thing had been very amusing. I thought so, too. But the organizer, a serious-minded little matron who had throughout regarded me with a very worried expression, took a different view. She was so ashamed that we could not assure her sufficiently of how glad we were to have participated. Even after we were installed in our tiny hotel room, she telephoned to ask whether she could not send us a quart of milk by way of refreshment.

After a visit to Montreal, we returned to New York, where a busy time awaited me. On the spot this time— that is to say, directly from BBC headquarters—I had to deliver a German broadcast. There was also a lecture to be given at Columbia University, and a speech to be prepared for the celebration of Alvin Johnson's seventieth birthday. Max Reinhardt had died. Because of a severe cold, I was unable to take part in the New York memorial meeting.

I was also chary of appearing because German exile circles, supported by Americans of German descent like Niebuhr, were much concerned with the Free Germany movement, and I was being asked to participate—even to take the leading role. The idea was to prepare a democratic German government that would be ready to take over after Hitler's inevitable collapse. Theologians, writers, socialist and Catholic statesmen belonged to the group, and it was suggested that I be placed at the head of it. "Idealists," wrote Felix Langer in his book *Stepping Stones to Peace*, "dream of Thomas Mann as the President of the second German Republic, a post that he himself would probably most decidedly refuse."

He was right. The idea of returning to a Germany become so alien to me, reduced by war to a state I could pretty well imagine, and there playing a political part

absolutely counter to my nature and profession, was anti-
pathetic to me to the depths of my soul. But I concurred
with the planners that any committee hoping to participate
in the shaping of Germany's future needed the sponsorship of the American government, just as the Paulus
group in Russia or the Czech government in exile in
England enjoyed such protection. And right at the outset
I expressed grave doubts as to whether the State Department would favour any organization that even remotely
resembled a German government in exile. Nevertheless,
I offered to go to Washington to clarify this crucial
question. I did so, and in a conversation with Assistant
Secretary of State Berle found my negative expectations
confirmed. With mixed feelings—for despite all my respect
for what my fellow countrymen were trying to do, this
dénouement was a relief to me—I reported the failure of
my mission at a second meeting.

At the theatre we saw Paul Robeson as Othello—good
and convincing in the beginning, inadequate later when
"chaos returns". His Desdemona was non-existent; the
Iago young, intelligent, but not made for that almost
allegorically ludicrous incarnation of absolute evil. In
company with our friend Caroline Newton, we also saw
a modern play. I was once again struck by the perfected
naturalness of the American theatre. It is not a question of
naturalism, which is a style. On the contrary, it is utter
unstylization, the enjoyment of reality, and is more lack of
inhibitions than art. A European actor, even a second-
rank one, stands out in such a troupe as a fascinating
foreign body. I must also not forget a glorious matinée
performance by the Busch Quartet at Town Hall—they
played Beethoven's Opus 132, that supreme work which,
by what might be called the kindness of providence, I

had the chance to hear at least five times during the years I was working on *Faustus*.

Early in December we set out for the Middle West, going first to Cincinnati so that I could keep a reading engagement at the university, and then—travelling in wartime discomfort—to St. Louis and Kansas City. There, at the house of Mr. Dekker, president of the University of Kansas City, we were joined by our eldest son, Klaus, a soldier in the American army, on the point of leaving for overseas, that is to say, for the European theatre of war. He preceded his brother Golo, who was still at the stage of basic training. Erika was with us; she, too, was determined to return to Europe to resume her activity as war correspondent. So we were together with these dear children for one last time before a parting that, presumably, might be for very long.

And so at last, after many adventures, efforts, achievements, we returned home by the most direct route. During all that time, in all the places we had been, I think I may say that the novel had never been absent from my thoughts for a moment. From Dr. Martin Gumpert I had obtained medical works on syphilis of the central nervous system. As I looked over these books during the trip, I was again reminded of how long this project had had to stand in line waiting its turn, waiting for the "fullness of time". I recalled that as early as 1905—four years, that is, after the earliest note about a Faust story—I had asked the bookseller Schüler on Maximilianstrasse in Munich about such literature. I remembered that my query had startled the good man. From the way he raised his eyebrows, it was clear he thought I had an all too personal interest in the subject.

Altogether, my reading on trains and in hotel rooms

was entirely related in some way or other to the book. Nothing else concerned me or could hold my attention— except, if it may be called an exception, newspaper accounts of current happenings, which were Zeitblom's affair as well as mine: the Moscow conference of Hull, Eden and Molotov, say, and corresponding politico-military emergency meetings of Marshal Keitel and his cronies. A volume of sixteenth-century humorous tales had accompanied me—for my narrative always stood with one foot in that century; parts of it would have to be cast in the language of the period, and in leisure hours en route I busied myself extracting older German words and phrases. I read Marlowe's *Faustus* and a German book on Riemenschneider in the Peasants' War. It is good, if we are bent upon serious achievement in narration, to keep in touch with great epical writing, to steep ourselves in its waters, so to speak. And so I read Jeremias Gotthelf, whose *Schwarze Spinne* (*The Black Spider*) I admire almost more than anything else in world literature. I read his *Uli der Knecht* (*Uli the Hired Man*), with its often Homeric overtones, and its paler postlude, *Uli der Pächter* (*Uli the Tenant Farmer*).

Music, too, of course, could not be left aside. I had kept with me both Berlioz' memoirs and Adorno's manuscript on Schönberg. His rigorous manner of veneration, the tragically cerebral relentlessness of his criticism of the contemporary musical situation, was precisely what I needed. For what I could draw from it, and what I appropriated from it in order to portray the whole cultural crisis in addition to the crisis of music, was the fundamental motif of my book: the closeness of sterility, the innate despair that prepares the ground for a pact with the devil. Moreover, this reading nourished the musical conception which had long been my ideal of form and for which this time there was a special aesthetic necessity. I felt clearly that my book itself would have to become the thing it dealt with: namely, a musical composition.

With some astonishment, but not without emotion, I reread what I had written in my journal on the journey from Denver to Los Angeles while the train rocked under me: "May the novel clarify and take proper form this winter! The first task is to remove all errors from the lecture chapter. A difficult work of art, like battle, peril at sea, or danger to life, brings us close to God in that it fosters a religious mood, and makes us raise our eyes reverently in an appeal for blessing, help, grace."

VII

Home-coming is a lovely adventure, especially home-coming to this Pacific Coast. I was enchanted by the light, by the special fragrance of the air, by the blue of the sky, the sun, the exhilarating ocean breeze, the spruceness and cleanliness of this southland. To ride once more over the stretch from railroad station to home (almost an hour's journey), with as much impending as when you went the same way in the reverse direction, has something improbable about it. You "never would have thought of it" quite like that. Faithful neighbours who had been keeping an eye on our things and taking care of the mail brought a huge sack of letters, along with cream, cake, and flowers. The Alfred Neumanns delivered the poodle who had been left with them and who now wavered, bewildered, between two sets of masters. In order to lose no time putting things on an orderly basis, you overtire yourself sifting through and destroying the accumulated printed matter, classifying letters brought along or waiting at home. One letter was from Bert Brecht, taking me to task for my lack of faith in German democracy. In what way had I shown it, this lack of faith? And was the charge justified? Perhaps my thought was that a terrible amount had still to be done before there would be any German democracy to discuss. To be sure, Hitler was the only one who did not know that he was lost, despite the fact that all Europe except for Italy was still in his hands. Consequently, we had the right to think beyond his foreseeable end. But how should we go about it?

Shortly after my return I had to deal with a letter from a news syndicate. They wished me to do an article for the *London Evening Standard* on the question of "What to Do with Germany". My inner monologue ran: "Precarious, carrying much responsibility, and at the same time unnecessary. Very likely this particular concern will be eliminated by unforeseen developments. What revolutionized, proletarianized, naked and stripped, shattered masses believing in nothing we shall have to deal with after this war. Proclamation of a national Bolshevism and a going over to Russia are not out of the question. This country is lost for a decent, liberal-democratic republic. . . ."

I did not write the article. My next task, undertaken gladly and with feelings of thankful remembrance, was to work up a speech for the Max Reinhardt memorial meeting, which took place on December 15 in the Wilshire Ebell Theatre in Los Angeles. That was probably the first time that the two women who had shared his life, Helene Thimig and Else Heims, found themselves together in the same room. Korngold and Szigeti played. Parts of the film of *A Midsummer Night's Dream* were shown. Fellow artists and pupils spoke, among them an American squirt eleven or twelve years of age, from Reinhardt's Hollywood theatre school, who gave us a sample of typical American ingenuousness and straightforwardness in public speaking which was almost comedy. "I don't know how to speak about Max in a solemn way. We simply were good friends. . . ." We concluded the evening with the Franks at the Brown Derby, but neither private nor public affairs seemed able to provide brighter material for our conversation. Franz Werfel's condition was causing us the gravest concern. And prospects for the war in Europe once again seemed dark and dubious. The disastrous episode at Bari had just been made public. Winston Churchill was ill in Egypt, suffering from his second bout of pneumonia.

I had begun work again on the revisions of Chapter VIII, gave it a new final form, and decided that I had it right at last. I resumed Chapter IX, which I had begun only to turn back once more to make further revisions on the earlier chapter. My aesthetic conscience was never to be fully satisfied with that bothersome section. Much later I again rewrote the final dialogue. At the end of the year I was in the midst of the next chapter. "Working on IX, and cut. Doubts about the composition. To be changed. Reminiscences of thematic material. . . . Frightful bombing of Berlin. . . . Reading Schönberg's *Harmony*. . . . Begun to write German broadcast. . . . The mail has brought a surprise order to appear for naturalization exam. . . . Read parts of *Lessons in Citizenship*."

On December 31: "We unite in the heartfelt wish that in the wild year to come our sons may both be safe. On the first day of the new year I must again take up work on the perhaps impossible novel. May something worthy be made of it!"

Only a few days of 1944 had passed when a memorable letter from Werfel arrived. Dictated from his sick-bed—which might be his death-bed. He spoke of *Buddenbrooks*, which he had just reread in three days and which he called, in the most earnest manner, an "immortal masterpiece". Although this work of my youth had for so long—almost half a century now—been leading its own life independent of me, and although it scarcely seemed to pertain to me any longer, I was deeply affected by this message, reaching me as it did under such curious circumstances. For my present undertaking was something like a belated return and home-coming to the old-fashioned German and musical sphere of that first novel. That *Buddenbrooks* should once more have captivated a first-rate artist's mind like Werfel's at this time of all times was bound to touch me deeply. For the rest, the considerations aroused by the letter were far from arrogant. "I am wondering," I wrote, "whether this book may not be the very one among all my works which is destined to survive. Perhaps my 'mission' was fulfilled in the writing of it, and it has been my lot only to fill the rest of a long life in a tolerably dignified and interesting manner. I do not want to be ungrateful and denigrate the course of my life, after that youthful cast of the die, as it developed through *The Magic Mountain*, *Joseph*, and *Lotte in Weimar*. But this might be a case like that of the *Freischütz*—that opera alone has remained alive among the people, although the composer followed it up by a good deal of music that was even better, nobler. Still and all, *Oberon* and *Euryanthe* are also in the repertoire. . . ."

A few days later I went to see Werfel, who looked very ill but immediately began to play oral variations upon the eulogies in his letter. I stood at the foot of his bed, beside which the oxygen apparatus was mounted. With eyes fixed upon me he explained that it seemed almost incredible to him to see the author of *Buddenbrooks* standing so materially before him. . . .

How characteristic of him was the childlikeness of this enthusiasm. I have always been very fond of Franz Werfel. I have admired his great lyrical gift as a poet and cherished his always interesting narrative art, although at times it lacks artistic self-control. I had my doubts about his playing with miracles in *Bernadette*—intellectually there is something impure about it. But I could never really blame his naïve and richly talented artistic nature for the mystical inclinations that more and more took root in him: for his flirting with Rome, his pious weakness for Church and Vatican. None of that bothered me except at those unfortunate moments when he became aggressively argumentative about it. At bottom he was a figure out of opera; he could even look like an opera singer (which it had once been his ambition to be), though at the same time he had the look of a Catholic priest. He had steadfastly rejected the temptation to become a convert, on the grounds that it would not do for him to deny his Judaism at a time of Jewish martyrdom. While he was "miserably recovering" from this, his second, heart attack and was spending a more or less solitary time in Santa Barbara finishing his utopian novel—that strange and as it were posthumous work—I was able to make him acquainted with some parts of the growing *Faustus* and to be warmed by his eager sympathy. We had dined at Romanoff's with Alma Mahler and then joined him, he having eaten at home with his personal physician. Lying on the sofa, he listened to my first three chapters, and I shall never forget how struck he was—or shall I say premonitively disturbed—by Adrian's *laughter*, in which he instantly recognized something of the uncanny, an element of religious diabolism. He asked about it again and again. "The laughter!" he said. "What are you getting at there? Oh, I know, I know. . . . We shall see." With insight and foresight, he thus picked out one of the small motifs of the book, the kind I most enjoy working with—like, say, the erotic motif of the blue and black eyes; the mother motif; the parallelism of the landscapes; or, more significant and essential, ranging through the whole book and appearing in many variations, the motif of cold, which is related to the motif of laughter.

In that laughter the devil, as the secret hero of the book, is invisibly present. He is there too in the "experiments" of Leverkühn's father, and my task was slowly to provide outlines for what could be sensed from the beginning, to allow it more and more to assume form and presence, as is done in the chapters on theology at Halle—first of all by Professor Kumpf's caricature of Luther (which is at the same time a comic prelude to the linguistic devices of the book, so that later on the Old German is really in every case a quote from Kumpf), and then by Schleppfuss' shady colleague. I had advanced into this region of the book by the middle of February. And although an article paying tribute to Bruno Walter on his fiftieth anniversary as a conductor was not the only interruption to the book, I had the witch story done, and also Chapter XIII, by the beginning of March. My comment: "Little satisfaction in the work, which seems to be dissolving under my hands. Certainly it is an original enterprise, but I doubt that my strength will suffice. A misguided idea to let it assume forms and dimensions akin to *The Magic Mountain*. The basis of that is fatigue and sluggishness."

This worry over the book's formlessness crops up repeatedly in the accompanying notes and the balance sheets I drew up for my own benefit. Cyril Connolly once commented perceptively that one must not be too vain to do a thing badly, and not too craven to admit it. Well, I am brave enough to admit that I was horrified at the prospect of bungling a major work and that I often suffered to the point of despair from the belief that I was actually doing so. Ultimately it was this "vanity" which conquered the fatigue and sluggishness and made of the novel the solid, coherent structure that it is.

I talked with Adorno whenever we met socially, and through these conversations I attempted to get a firmer grip on the musical problems of the book. I was already concerned about the idea of the "breakthrough", which was greatly in need of clarification. With sympathetic interest and eagerness to help in any way he could, Adorno brought me a highly pertinent book on Alban Berg, who was born in the same year as Adrian (1885)—and with whom, incidentally, I had once corresponded. I had completely forgotten this, probably because I had not then clearly grasped his importance. Alma Mahler had to remind me that after the publication of the first volume of *Joseph and His Brothers* he had written a very cordial letter to me from Vienna, and that I had replied gratefully. I would give a great deal to have his letter still. With so much else, it was left by the wayside.

A memorable literary event occurred while I was working on Chapter XIV—the student talks, for which, incidentally, I used a document that I found among my various old papers, a German youth magazine published by the Wandervögel or some similar group. The literary event, which for days concerned me in the deepest and most personal way, was the arrival from Switzerland of both volumes of Hermann Hesse's *Glasperlenspiel*. After years of work, my friend in distant Montagnola had completed this difficult and beautiful novel of his old age, of which I had hitherto seen only the magnificent introduction that had come out in the *Neue Rundschau*. I had often said that this writing was as close to me "as if it were part of myself", as it goes in the old poem, *I Had a Comrade*. Now, seeing the whole thing, I was almost alarmed at its kinship with the task I had elected: the same idea of fictional biography—with the dashes of parody that this form necessarily involves; the same connection with music. Also, a criticism of culture and our era, although from the point of view of a visionary cultural utopia and theory of culture rather than of a passionate and telling dramatization of our tragedy. With all the differences, there remained a disturbing similarity. My diary note, "To be reminded that one is not alone in the world— always unpleasant," bluntly renders this aspect of my feelings. It is another version of the question in Goethe's *Westöstlicher Diwan*: "Do we then live if others live?" and is also reminiscent of certain remarks by Saul Fitelberg on the unwillingness of artists to know about one another —remarks that I later wrote without applying them to myself.

I admit to a wholehearted contempt for mediocrity. The mediocre know nothing of excellence and therefore lead an easy, stupid life. To my mind, too many people write. But with those who tread the same difficult path, I think I may call myself a good colleague who does not look grudgingly at the good and great things that are being done alongside him, and who is far too fond of admiration, and believes in it far too deeply, to reserve his own for the dead.

I was face to face with mature excellence here. Certainly much effort, deeply concealed and carefully applied, had gone into this work. With what humour and artistry had these contrived to keep the intellectualization that comes with old age within the bounds of concreteness and playfulness. I knew scarcely another work which inspired such warm and respectful feelings of comradeship in me. That I should compare and contrast my own work with this one, whose mastery I had acknowledged, was perfectly compatible with such feelings.

"Evening, reading Hesse's novel. *Magister Thomas von der Trave* and *Joseph Knecht*. Their different ways of handling the bead game prettily delineated. . . . The parallels between the broader themes of the books astonishing. Mine probably more pointed, sharper, more searing, more dramatic (because more dialectical), more topical and direct. His softer, more sentimental, more self-sufficient, more romantic, and more playful (in a high sense). His approach to music marked by pious antiquarianism. Nothing fine after Purcell. Amorous pleasures and suffering entirely excluded from this 'novel' and indeed scarcely conceivable in it. The conclusion, Knecht's death, delicately homoerotic. The intellectual horizon, the cultural content, very broad. Along with that a great deal of jesting in the style of the biographical researcher; use of comical names." I wrote to Hesse particularly about this, the humorous side of his book, and he was pleased with my stressing it.

Our youngest daughter, the wife of Antonio Borgese, had had her second baby, and we spent two weeks in

Chicago, our trip lasting into April. In dark weather, amid gusts of snow, I tried, in our lakeside hotel, to push the current chapter forward, and along with this took care of a new broadcast to Germany—it dealt with the air raids and the question of conscience posed by them. The German edition of *Joseph the Provider* had recently been published, and Bermann sent me a number of Swiss reviews of the book, pro and con. This way of devouring, as it were in a lump, public comment on work that one has already placed behind one is confusing, annoying, and futile in the extreme. Of course we are grateful when someone occasionally makes a good and intelligent point on a work whose merits and frailties we know only too well. But we become ashamed of the avidity with which we indulge in this unwholesome pleasure, and afterwards the craving to live in new things is all the stronger. I continued to follow up the wooing motif in Shakespeare; I read *Measure for Measure* and then Flaubert's *Saint Anthony*—with amazement at the polyhistorical nihilism of this magnificent work, which at bottom is only a fantastic catalogue of all human idiocies. "A long review of the insanity of the religious world—and then, at the end, the countenance of Christ? Dubious." Ivan Karamazov's vision of the devil was also included in my reading at the time. I read the scene with the same sort of distant attentiveness with which I had reread *Salammbô* again before beginning on the *Joseph*.

Once again back home, we heard that Bruno Frank, too, had had a severe heart attack and was still bedridden. Heart attack, in the form of coronary thrombosis or angina pectoris, is the most frequently mentioned cause of illness and death among Americans; but the exiles seemed to be particularly susceptible to it—which is scarcely to be wondered at. At the same time Schönberg and Döblin were suffering from asthmatic conditions of cardiac origin. I paid Döblin a sick-bed visit. Not long afterwards Martin Gumpert nearly succumbed to a dangerous attack. One after the other these men, given a conditional reprieve of their death sentence, had sworn off cigarettes. "I must regard myself as still in splendid shape," I noted in the diary. In point of fact I myself was feeling rather awful. Under the impact of icy Chicago winds, a catarrh had settled upon me. It produced snuffles, bronchitis, sinusitis, and a general feeling of illness and needed medical attention. Easter I was confined to my bedroom, dosing myself with cough medicine and nose and throat sprays; but almost immediately I went on again, pressing forward in the novel. By the middle of April I completed Chapter XIV and went right on to the next, which I finished in ten days, with Luther's letters and Grimmelshausen's *Simplicissimus* as accompanying reading matter. That chapter contains the correspondence between Adrian and Kretschmar and, in Adrian's letter, the undeclared reproduction of the third *Meistersinger* prelude, which gave me great pleasure.

The Russians had just taken Odessa. The German official line now was that "the enemy is incapable of interfering with our regrouping operation". Instead, the Russians turned upon Sebastopol, which now became the focal point of struggle. Almost every day now there were reports of colossal air raids upon "Fortress Europe"—a concept largely fabricated by German propaganda. The explosions along the invasion coast made houses in England shake. General Perkins[1] stated that the coming landing would tie up the German troops in the West and

---

[1] This officer could not be identified more closely. (Publisher's Note)

give the Russians a free hand for their offensive. They were to reach Berlin first. The landing, incidentally, was technically almost inconceivable, he said, and the cost in manpower was estimated at half a million.

The Germans had marched into Hungary as if this were 1939, and were intensifying their reign of terror in Denmark. But at the same time there were clear signs that they were losing hope of victory. The speeches of Goebbels and Goering on Hitler's birthday had the sound of a cracked dish. The *Schwarze Korps*, which I had always found particularly repugnant because of a certain literary finish and smartness about it, published a sneering article on the possible resurrection of the Weimar Republic, the return of Bruening, Albert Greszinsky, Einstein, Weiss —and myself. I swore to myself that they would never catch a glimpse of me.

Erika read to us from her delightful book of memoirs, *Alien Homeland*, reawakening many vivid recollections of 1933. She had an article in the *Aufbau* arguing, I thought rightly, against the *émigré* patriotism of the group associated with "Democratic Germany", whose desire it was to see Germany once more "free" and great after the war, who were against any forfeiting of territory and even wanted to keep the partnership of Austria and Germany. Wittingly or unwittingly—and this was my reason for rejecting them—they were making common cause with a sinister pro-Germanism very much alive everywhere, which might better have been called pro-Fascism. Typical of this attitude was a letter to me from some professor of literature in Ohio, who accused me of being responsible for the war. "Even a piece of arrant folly is a stab at the heart," I wrote.

We had, as I had hoped, come to see much more of

Stravinsky and his wife—a thoroughgoing *belle Russe*, that is to say, an example of that specifically Russian beauty that radiates the most likeable of human qualities. Talking with him at an evening gathering in our house, I was struck by things he said—with Gide as a starting point, and speaking alternately in German, English and French— concerning *confession* as the product of various cultural spheres: the Greek Orthodox, the Roman Catholic, and the Protestant. In his opinion Tolstoy was essentially German and Protestant.

I do not remember who called my attention to Voltaire's *Mahomet*, which I now read for the first time in Goethe's translation—impressed by the parade of types and characters of enormous historical significance to be found in this brilliant piece of work. I also occupied myself with a curious old book *Musikalische Briefe eines Wohlbekannten* (*Musical Letters of a Well-Known Man*) (Leipzig, 1852), which I had picked up somewhere. The thing itself was utterly comic, a perfect specimen of culture of the bourgeois age, the very tone of the well-read philistine abominated by Nietzsche. Nevertheless, in spite of its fantastic *naïveté*, there were many useful items to be garnered from it, for example on Mendelssohn.

Work on the novel, in spite of many a weary hour, many a spell of depression, springing from the "consciousness of writing falsely", had now regained something of its initial impetus. Was this because "my season" had come—May and June, the season of my birth, when there was usually an upswing in my vital forces? Chapter XVI, with Adrian's letter from Leipzig, which introduces in montage Nietzsche's adventure in the Cologne bordello, and Chapter XVII, in which the letter is analysed by his anxious friend, followed one another in quick succession.

I had escaped from the tangle of motifs in the expositional part of the book and saw clear action before me. An easy matter to tell the story of the painful love affair with the poisonous butterfly, to introduce the note cipher h, e, a, e, e-flat, to sketch in the strange ill luck that attended Adrian's visits to the doctors, since I had already prepared the reader for all this.

On the morning of June 6, my sixty-ninth birthday, Agnes Meyer telephoned from Washington, before I had even glanced at the newspapers, not only to bestow her congratulations but to tell me the news that the invasion of France had begun. She had received gratifying reports directly from the War Department. It was a moment of great emotion, and looking back upon the adventures of these eleven years I could not help but see a meaningful dispensation, one of the harmonies of my life, in the fact that the longed-for, the scarcely-thought-possible event, was taking place on this day, my day. Naturally thoughts of the invasion, and the earnest hope that it would continue to go well, overshadowed all the festive gaieties the day brought me. With visitors we discussed the landing. The telephone kept ringing without pause. Yet it is worth recording that even on this day, though repeatedly called away from my desk, I pushed the novel forward by very nearly my normal daily stint. In the evening we had the Werfels and the Franks. "Conversation on the world of the book." Then: "At eleven o'clock listened to detailed invasion reports from Hollywood and London."

VIII

Friday, June 23, 1944, was, as I wrote at the time, "a memorable day in this span of eleven years". We rose very early and right after breakfast drove to the Federal Building in Los Angeles. There we were admitted into a crowded hall where an official was issuing instructions. The judge appeared, sat down on one of the chairs upon the platform, and made a little speech whose admirable form and kindly content surely reached into other hearts as well as mine. We rose to take the oath jointly and then went individually to another place to sign the citizenship papers. So we were now American citizens, and I am glad to think—but had best be brief in uttering this thought—that I became one under Roosevelt, in *his* America.

I kept turning back from later sections of the book to Adrian's Leipzig letter, a *tour de force* and one of the sore points of the novel. I was dissatisfied with it and was for ever making changes. "However I do it, it is wrong. Am I forced to dry out the material and so spoil it?" There were moments—at times protracted ones—of terrible weariness. Perhaps declining health and too-low blood pressure—one of the less agreeable effects of the California climate—were to blame. I had no appetite, was dyspeptic, dull, and hypercritical of everything I did. The doctor prescribed atropine and vitamin injections— the sort of thing which, in my experience, is only useful in that the patient has the illusion something is being done. Far more effectual was the news from Cherbourg, and stories like that of the German general and admiral who went and surrendered, after dispatching the usual heroic radiograms to the Führer. The two had simply decamped, leaving their troops behind with orders to fight to the last man. The invading forces were already fighting around Caen; fundamentally, the battle for Paris was already on. In the East, Minsk was on the verge of falling; and after this city had been taken, the Russians began an advance whose rapidity was almost uncanny. They had only to come near and the strongest fortresses (Lvov, Brest Litovsk) fell like ripe plums. Schönberg, and he was not the only one among my acquaintances, was firmly convinced that this was all pre-arranged, that an agreement had been reached. This alone, he reasoned, explained the contrast between the stubborn German defence in Italy and France and the precipitate retreat in the East. But after all that had happened, was any understanding between the Russians and the German régime conceivable? I had often considered the possibility that Germany might seek her only way out by throwing herself into the arms of Russia. But it seemed most unlikely that this choice was still open to her, and so I found this relatively widespread theory fantastic. Incidentally, within the Reich, while the robots wreaked havoc on England, Goebbels was calling for peace with the Anglo-Saxons, was ranting at Russia and following the tried-and-true formula, which this time did not work, of staking everything on the fear of Bolshevism.

Sainte-Beuve's marvellous essay on Molière came my way for the first time at just this period. It is a brilliant piece of critical beatification, assisted by all the heavenly hosts of French tradition and culture. The equivocal position of the writer-actor in his time and society, a position that must have been very like that of Shakespeare, is most movingly painted. Louis XVI served Molière pheasant, but the royal officers considered him unworthy company, and even Boileau regretted his "touch of the jester". Sainte-Beuve ranks him with the five or six geniuses of the world who worked between primitive and civilized, Homeric and Alexandrine epochs. Naïve, but already extremely clever, these were geniuses who in richness, fertility, and deftness surpass the very greatest, says Sainte-Beuve. It is plain that he does not count Goethe among these. Goethe himself would probably not have done so; otherwise he would not, all his life, have regarded Shakespeare as so far above himself. But there are judgments on Goethe in this French critic which strike the German ear as curiously sharp, though not inaccurate. Thus, Sainte-Beuve speaks of Molière's composure, self-control, coolness, and lucidity in the midst of ardour. This cool-headedness in the midst of the most emotional drama, he says, has nothing in common with the calculated, icy impartiality to be found in Goethe, that "Talleyrand of art", "Such intellectual refinements within the realm of poesy were still unknown." As for Goethe being in some sense a "Talleyrand", Byron too called him "an old fox"—this on the basis of *The Elective Affinities*.

A Swiss journal had an article on the French poet St. John-Perse; I noted his verdict on Voltaire's *Charles XII*: "Excellent, but not great." A noteworthy distinction! . . . It was Jacob Burckhardt who said of Voltaire: "In him rationalism becomes poetic, even mythic." I should like to see the German writer who could produce such a sentence! Switzerland is the country in which the most gloriously un-German things are said in German. That is why I love it.

I now started to learn a good deal about Kierkegaard,

strangely enough before I took up reading him directly. Adorno had given me his weighty essay on K. I studied it along with the brilliant essay by Georg Brandes. One passage in Kierkegaard which I copied out reads: "The humorist constantly relates the concept of God to something else, and brings out the contradiction, but does not relate himself to God in religious passion (*stricte sic dictus*). He transforms himself into a jesting and profound passageway for this whole transaction, but has no relationship of his own to God." K'.s style, at least in German, is not good. But how new and profound is this definition of humour! What superlatively intelligent observation!

Evenings, I listened to music on the radio or record player with extreme and objective attentiveness. Fortune had it that we could enjoy chamber music right in our own house. The Dutch 'cellist Vandenburg and the violinists Temianka and Pollack visited and with one or another of our friends, occasionally before a group of guests, played quartets of Haydn, Mozart, Beethoven (Opus 132!), Mendelssohn, Brahms, and Dvořak. Michael, our youngest son, once again came with his family and joined in as violist. Frido appeared, with his hair cut for the first time. "Drew for the little fellow," is a frequent notation in my journal. "Frido, nervous and a bit fractious, with me a great deal."

The Russians were outside Warsaw, threatening Memel. In Paris the Germans, with the aid of the collaborationists, were warring against the increasingly bold Résistance. Terrible reports came through on the growing massacre of the Jews; then accounts of the generals' attempt to assassinate Hitler, of the failure of the coup, the mass execution of army officers, the complete Nazification of the

army, and a kind of general mobilization of the people—
Goebbels' "total war".

At this time I sent off a long letter to President Beneš,
telling him my reasons for becoming an American citizen
and giving up Czech citizenship. I received the kindliest
of replies. The next thing to do in the novel was the portrait
of Rüdiger Schildknapp. It turned out an artistically suc-
cessful bit, and at that time I was not even conscious of its
recklessness in human terms—for it was a portrait, though
a highly stylized one which differs in essential details from
its model. Moreover, Europe, Germany, and all who
lived there—or no longer lived—were separated by too
deep and ultimate a gulf, were too submerged, belonged
too much to the past and to dreams—were submerged,
lost, vanished by their own will. So, too, was the figure of
that friend whom I invoked with apparent exactitude,
but actually with much trimmed away. Besides, I was still
far too greatly under the spell of a work that was confession
and sacrifice through and through and hence would not be
bound by considerations of mere discretion, a work that
took the form of the most disciplined art and at the same
time stepped out of art and became reality. And yet this
reality in its turn referred back to the work itself, it was
responsible in certain cases more to form than to truth, was
metaphorical and phantasmal. In a very competent German
review of the book (in *Dramaturgische Blätter*) Paul Rilla
was later to write: "The writer of these notes was joyously
surprised to discover the portrait of a friend in the book,
an engaging writer and translator, unmistakable in every
feature, astonishingly apt in every gesture. . . ." Well,
the interested party would have thought differently, and
did think differently, about the unmistakability of the
picture. I must here pay him the tribute of recording that

73

he took the whole thing in the most generous spirit and displayed only the faintest sensitivity at having been made a character in my novel.

After I had read aloud from the book one evening, Leonhard Frank asked me whether I had had any model in mind for Adrian himself. I said no, and added that the difficulty consisted precisely in inventing the biography of a musician who could then take his place among the real situations and personalities of modern musical life. Leverkühn was, I said, a kind of ideal figure, a "hero of our time", a person who bore the suffering of the epoch. I went further, however, and confessed that I had never loved a creature of my imagination—neither Thomas Buddenbrook, nor Hans Castorp, nor Aschenbach, nor Joseph, nor the Goethe of *Lotte in Weimar*—as I did Adrian. The only exception, perhaps, was Hanno Buddenbrook. I was telling the truth. Quite literally I shared good Serenus' feelings for him, was painfully in love with him from his days as an arrogant schoolboy, was infatuated with his " coldness", his remoteness from life, his lack of "soul"—that mediator and conciliator between spirit and instinct—with his "inhumanity" and his "despairing heart", with his conviction that he was damned. At the same time, oddly enough, I scarcely gave him any appearance, any physical body. My family was always wanting me to describe him. If the narrator had to be reduced to a mere figment, a kind heart and a hand trembling as it held the pen, well and good. But at least I should make his hero and mine visible, should give him a physical individuality, should make it possible for the reader to picture him. How easily that could have been done! And yet how mysteriously forbidden it was, how impossible, in a way I had never felt before! Impossible in a different sense from the impossibility of Zeitblom's describing himself. Here there was a prohibition to be kept—or, at any rate, a commandment of maximum restraint. To depict Adrian's outer appearance was instantly to threaten him with spiritual downfall, to undermine his symbolic dignity, to diminish and render banal his representativeness. That was the way it was. Only the characters more remote from the centre of the book could be novelistic figures in the picturesque sense—all the Schildknapps, Schwerdtfegers, Roddes, Schlaginhaufens, etc. But not the two protagonists, who had too much to conceal, namely, the secret of their being identical with each other.

The summer weeks, during which I worked on the chapters preceding Adrian's removal to Munich, brought us a visit of importance to me. Ernst Křenek and his wife came to stay, and I was able to thank him for *Music Here and Now*. On our walk under the palm trees of Ocean Avenue, and afterwards at our house, I was able to learn a great deal of value from him on the fate of music in the past forty years, its present status, the relationship of the public and the various types of soloists and conductors to its new forms. Books such as *Music, a Science and Art*, by Redfield; *The Musical Scene*, by Virgil Thomson; *The Book of Modern Composers*, by David Ewen; and especially Ernest Newman's *The Unconscious Beethoven* supplemented such tutelage. I read with careful attention a book that was not directly pertinent, but whose keen analysis stimulated me to consider the situation of the novel in general and where I myself stood in its history. This was *James Joyce*, by Harry Levin. Since I cannot have direct access to the linguistic structure erected by the Irish writer, I have had to depend upon the critics for elucidation of the phenomenon he presents. Books like Levin's, and Campbell's and Robinson's major commentary on *Finnegans Wake*, have revealed to me many an unexpected relationship and—given such vast difference in our literary natures—even affinity. I had held the prejudice that alongside Joyce's eccentric avant-gardism my work was bound to seem like lukewarm traditionalism. To be sure, this much is true: a link with tradition, no matter how parodistic that link is, makes for easier accessibility, opens the way for a degree of popularity. But this is more a matter of attitude than of essence. "As his subject matter reveals the decomposition of the middle class," Levin writes, "Joyce's technique passes beyond the limits of English realistic fiction. Neither *A Portrait of the Artist* nor *Finnegans Wake* is a novel, strictly speaking, and *Ulysses* is a novel to end all novels." This probably applies to *The Magic Mountain*, the *Joseph* story, and equally well to *Doctor Faustus*. T. S. Eliot's question "whether the novel had not outlived its function since Flaubert and James, and whether *Ulysses* should not be considered an epic" paralleled my own question whether in the field of the novel nowadays the only thing that counted was what was no longer a novel. There are sentences in Levin's book which touched me with a strange intensity. "The best writing of our contemporaries is not an act of creation, but an act of evocation, peculiarly saturated with reminiscences." And this other one: "He has enormously increased the difficulties of being a novelist."

"Difficulty with the chapter. Must keep back certain cherished items that would overload the book and seem too material. Idea of having the devil appear in threefold guise, always wrapped in icy cold. . . . Last part rewritten. *Meilleur*. Attacked XXI again. Notes for the conversation with the devil. Writing away on XXII (twelve-tone system). Felt deep enjoyment at integrating material studied and assimilated into the atmosphere and context of the book. . . ."

It moved forward, despite any waverings of my faith. Towards the end of August—Paris had been taken, the German garrison driven out, Laval was in flight, Pétain kidnapped by the Germans—I regarded the novel as "half written" and felt that I could permit myself an interruption—one reason being, no doubt, that I had contracted with the Colston Leigh agency for a lecture tour and had to prepare for it. However, I wrote to them asking to have my itinerary shortened, for I shrank from expending too much energy on distant travels. I worked on some small incidental pieces: a foreword to the Stockholm edition of Bruno Frank's *Cervantes* and an article on Grimmelshausen for another Swedish publisher. Meanwhile I listened to Leonhard Frank's readings, at evening visits, from his *Deutsche Novelle* (*A German Story*). He was in the odd situation of being unable to conclude his novel *Mathilde* until he saw how the war ended. Therefore he was profitably whiling away the time with the shaping of this smaller work. No doubt it had gathered up all sorts of elements from the spirit of *Faustus*—moods and ideas, which, incidentally, belonged to him just as much as they did to me. I was alarmed by the title. The word *German* was used in jest, to be sure. But whereas I had to put it into the sub-title as a mere unemotional attributive of *composer*, he was blatantly displaying it in the principal title, indeed was making it the title itself. Good though he usually was about accepting advice and criticism of details, in this matter he would not be swayed by any appeal to taste and discretion. I listened to his low-voiced, slightly hesitant reading with deep appreciation. The perfect picture of the old German town (Rothenburg ob der Tauber); the craft elements, which Frank knew intimately from his youth as mechanic and locksmith's apprentice and to which he contrived to give a specifically German nimbus; the painful psychological theme underlying the story, namely, the parting of the ways between sexuality and eroticism; and the secretly demonic quality of the whole—all this exerted an extraordinary attraction upon me. I remain an admirer of this story, which has been undeservedly ignored, for it is a minor masterpiece.

Music again and again—by some mysterious means life and society continued to put it for ever at my beck and call. It came my way far more frequently than it does today when, the novel finished, music and matters related to it have once more moved out to the periphery of my interests. Through the Neumanns we met Dr. Albersheim, a musician and musicologist of conservative cast, whose opinions and attitudes were a far remove from Adorno's, and not as useful to my task. Nevertheless, we spent enjoyable evenings at Albersheim's, when he had rising instrumentalists and singers, "stars in the making", in for concerts. The violinist Henry Temianka lived far away, even beyond the Bowl in the downtown direction; but distance did not deter me, though at this season there was danger of fog on the homeward way. We heard that violin sonata of Handel which has the most beautiful of all larghettos; the Bach *partita* in eight movements; a quartet with oboe, which part however was taken by a violin, by a Hungarian composer who was there for the performance. We dined with Charles Laughton, the uncannily amusing and slyly deep actor, who afterwards did a magnificent recitation from *The Tempest* in his British English. Neither

78

Paris nor the Munich of 1900 could have provided an evening so rich in intimate artistic spirit, verve, and merriment.

About this time Adorno gave me his extremely shrewd treatise on Wagner to read. Its critical dichotomies and its somewhat stiff attitude towards the subject, which never entirely passes over to the negative side, give it a certain kinship with my own essay, *Sufferings and Greatness of Richard Wagner*. It was probably the reading of Adorno's essay that prompted me one evening to play once more the records of *Elsa's Träume*, with the magical interpolation of the *pianissimo* trumpet at the words, *"In lichter Waffen Schein—ein Ritter nahte da"*, and the closing scene of *Rheingold*, with its unfolding beauties and ingenuities: the first appearance of the sword theme, the wonderful manipulation of the Valhalla motif, Loki's brilliant and characteristic interjections, the *"Glänzt nicht mehr euch Mädchem das Gold"*, and above all the indescribably affecting *"Traulich und treu ist's nur in der Tiefe"* of the Rhine maidens' terzet. "The triad world of the *Ring*," my diary confesses, "is at bottom my musical homeland." However, I added: "And yet at the piano I never tire of the *Tristan* chord."

Incidentally, music was at this point not strictly pertinent, as far as plot was concerned, to the further course of the novel, on which I very soon resumed work. With Chapter XXIII I pressed forward into the social subsidiary plot, into recollections of Munich. I had the task before me of bringing Adrian to Pfeiffering and installing him in the Schweigestill household. There was probably some connection between this enterprise and my choosing to read Stendhal's letters. I was no little impressed by the intelligence, manliness, courage, and sensibility of the author of *Le Rouge et le Noir*—a novel that makes one feel that no novel ever existed before. I was particularly struck by his experience with the young Russian officer "whom he does not dare to look at". Otherwise passion would seize him "if" (the *if* is repeated), he, Stendhal, "were a woman". "What he was observing in himself were the labour pains of a passion. A rare irruption of homoeroticism in a markedly masculine personality, but one that was extremely open and curious about psychology. Of course I took note of the incident in connection with Adrian's relationship to Rudi Schwerdtfeger, which I had planted early in the book—Rudi lays siege to the would-be hermit and lures him into an intimacy in which the homosexual element plays an impish part.

Aldous Huxley's *Time Must Have a Stop* gave me extraordinary pleasure—it is without doubt an audacious, topranking performance in the contemporary novel. I read Nietzsche's *Ecce Homo* again, Bekker's *Beethoven* and Deussen's memoir, *Erinnerungen an Nietzsche*. Letters from the children overseas moved us—to concern and also to pride in our participating through them in the war that we felt was a struggle against the enemy of mankind. Klaus, who had had a friend almost literally snatched from his side by a shell during the fighting in Italy, was down with malaria in a British Army hospital. Golo, in London, was busy from morning to midnight working for the American Broadcasting Station in Europe. He made light as best he could, *ad usum parentum*, of the flying robots, which were still coming over. Erika was in Paris, witnessing the unrepentant state of mind of the French bourgeoisie and upper class—and the way the point of view of the liberators reinforced their attitude.

But the career of the Third Reich was speeding to its conclusion. Already the struggle had ceased to be for

"Fortress Europe" and was concentrating upon "Fortress Germany". German names began to appear in the communiqués of both sides. In East and West the Allies stood on German soil. What life the Nazi state still had left, it employed for ugly murders. Movies were actually made for the Führer recording the slow strangulation of the disloyal officers. General Rommel, who had also been involved in the plot, was given the choice between suicide with a state funeral or a humiliating treason trial followed by death on the gallows. He took poison and remained "the most important general of this war". Montgomery had always carried a picture of him and hoped some day to meet him face to face. There is little doubt that in sports-minded England Rommel would have been hailed as the tough, bold, and adroit opponent that he was. Had it been impossible for him to escape across the Channel? One felt it as a pity and vexation each time another man died for Hitler! . . . When Aachen lay buried in rubble and ashes, the Nazi bigwigs began eliminating one another.

Here at home we were anxious to assure Roosevelt's fourth term against the Republican candidate, and I was glad that the local party organization called upon me to take part in a public meeting for the man I so greatly admired. Alongside notes such as, "Working long and eagerly on the chapter," is to be found, towards the end of October, the item: "Speech for Roosevelt." The gathering took place on the afternoon of October 29 in a private garden in the Bel Air residential section. Only about two hundred persons came, but in spite of the fog and cold that set in towards evening they stuck it out for hours on chairs set up on the lawn, for everybody was "having a good time". On such occasions, it is the custom of the country for the political inspirational speeches and the money-raising (for which certain speakers have developed a fantastic technique) to be interlarded with all sorts of *variété* amusements which have nothing whatsoever to do with the cause but which none the less contribute to the political effectiveness of the affair after their fashion. Here they had, among others, an extremely skilful magician, allegedly Spanish, who claimed to have learned his magic from a great Chinese sage named Rosenthal, and a girl ventriloquist, quite young, yet expert in her art, who chatted so drolly with a pop-eyed doll on her lap that I was still laughing when I went up to the platform to make my speech—one obviously far too earnest for these circumstances. But it was not too earnest; it proved to be quite right—again, after its fashion. More comedy followed it, and in the end everyone had so thoroughly amused himself that no one had the slightest lingering doubt of F.D.R.'s re-election.

How strangely it touched me to read the brief diary note of the day immediately thereafter. I had once more returned to *Love's Labour's Lost* and copied out a couplet from the play:

> There form confounded makes most form in mirth;
> When great things labouring perish in their birth.

My notation was: "The first line may apply to *Joseph*, the second to *Faustus*." The quotation and comment would show me, should I have forgotten, with what scruples and doubts I had to contend all through the writing of the novel, how disposed I was to believe in its failure. These anxieties painfully increased in proportion to the decline in my health. Only two days later (during an evening gathering at Eddie Knopf's, with Ernst Lubitsch, Count Ostheim, his American wife, and Salka Viertel present) I was suffering from a severe headache, and the following morning I came down with a *grippe* that attacked stomach and intestines and in the course of a single week caused me to lose fourteen pounds—a loss of weight that I was not able to make up again for many months.

IX

I was out of bed in time for election day, November 7. But the infection, as it often is with me, was hard to expel. It continued to smoulder in the organism and produced unpleasant after-effects: a troublesome sore throat, then violent facial pains and psuedo toothache proceeding from the "triplex nerve", pains that gave me bad days and worse nights. The mixture of empirin and codeine was of little avail; I shifted to small heating pads of flaxseed and, in my fury at the neuralgia, applied them so ruthlessly that I gave myself serious burns of the mucus membrane of the mouth.

Along with all this it became necessary to rearrange my work. There was a lecture tour I had to prepare for, and I began looking around for a subject proper to the time and also to myself. It should be, I thought, as close as possible to my main occupation, my current work, to lean upon that as much as possible, and be derived from that—something about Germany, about the character and destiny of the German people. And amid all kinds of reading about German history, the Reformation, and the Thirty Years' War, and also dipping into Croce's *History of Europe*, I began making preliminary notes on this subject, although all the while I felt no real desire or resolve to continue with it. Any such change of the direction of my thoughts, the neces-

sity to find my way into new material, is always a troublesome matter that strains my nerves and in itself half brings
on illness. As things stood at the time, it was a threefold
burden. But my inner refractoriness could hardly be described as eagerness to return to my main task. "Protracted
psychological low, intensified by horror at the misguided-
ness of the novel that I began with so zestful a sense of
experiment. Heavy, inactive days." Then: "Dinner at the
Werfels, with the Franks, who have just returned from
their New York expedition. Frank the worse for wear
rather than refreshed. I read Chapter XXIII (Munich)
with great strain. Was surprised at sympathetic interest.
Intelligent, moving remarks by Werfel concerning the
thematic material and the unusual character of the book,
which seems to me so dangerously on the brink of failure."

This was probably decisive. The working hours of the
next day still went to sketching the lecture, but by the day
after, I had decided to postpone it and the trip indefinitely,
and to send the agent and MacLeish telegrams cancelling
my appearance on the grounds of ill health. "Difficult
decision which I have long dodged. It relieves me, of
course, but I also feel ashamed as if I were playing hooky
from school. And yet would not leaving the novel in mid-
air have come to precisely the same thing? The very fact
of my being so disturbed about this book, *which one way or
another must be brought to its conclusion*, is one more reason
not to let it be postponed by protracted labours on the
lecture and the trip. As I am writing, K. is sending the
telegrams. Empirin against the pains. . . ."

One way or another. Henceforth the entries read: "Occupied with *Faustus*. Preparatory work, linguistic and
objective, for the next chapter. . . . In the evening, once
again hours on Nietzsche's letters. Moved by the relation-

ship with Rohde, which on the other hand inexorably proceeds more and more towards a monstrous caricature of a relationship. One-sidedness and hopelessness of his connection with Burckhardt. The brief flash of hope in Brandes. Nietzsche's somewhat schoolboyish enthusiasm for the fact that the name 'Goethe' originally means the great outpourer, begetter, stallion—the man! . . . '' I wrote the transition chapter, XXIV, which is set in Palestrina, in fourteen days, and in between read to Adorno and his wife, and friends whom they had brought with them, the correspondence between Adrian and Kretschmar. The dialectical quality of this exchange appealed to the Hegelian in Adorno. But he praised even more the description of the music woven into the chapter, although curiously enough he did not recognize its model (the prelude to the third act of *Meistersinger*). He mistook the dimensions and imagined it a much longer piece of my own invention—which to my mind was quite all right. As far as I was concerned, the main thing was that I had once more put him into contact with the musical aspect of the book and had aroused his enthusiasm for it. Much as he revered Schönberg, he had no personal intercourse with him—the probable explanation being that the old man sensed the critical note within his disciple's respect. On the other hand, Hanns Eisler was to be met at Schönberg's house. I always took the greatest pleasure in Eisler's sparkling conversation, especially when it centred around Wagner and the comical ambivalence of Eisler's relationship to that great demagogue. Eisler would "catch on to his tricks", shake his finger in the air, and cry out: "You old fraud!" It made me shake with laughter. I recall how he and Schönberg one evening, at my urging incidentally, went through the *Parsifal* harmonic system at the piano, searching for unresolved dissonances. To be precise, there was only one: in the Amfortas part of the last act. They then explained archaic forms of variation, about which I had inquired for good reasons of my own, and Schönberg presented me with a pencilled sheet of notes and figures illustrating the matter.

Kierkegaard's *Either—Or* had come my way at the time, and I read it with close attention. "His mad love for Mozart's *Don Juan*. Sensuality, discovered by Christianity along with spirit. Music as a demonic realm, 'sensual genius'. . . . The novel's congruence to Kierkegaard's philosophy, of which I had had no knowledge, is most remarkable. The conversation on 'Mount Zion' on Christian marriage, say—and many other elements—would seem to presume a knowledge of K."

Towards the middle of December I began—with the notation, "whatever may come of it now"—Chapter XXV, the devil chapter, at the beginning of which Leverkühn sits in the Italian room, holding Kierkegaard's book in his hand. "Wrote away at conversation with the devil," now remains for two months, past Christmas and a good way into the new year, the standing entry for my day's activity—amid the alternations of life, the happenings of the war, the ups and downs of my health, and also the inevitable diversions from work, of which I shall only mention two: the radio broadcasts to Germany, still due every once in a while—I would drive out to the National Broadcasting Company offices in Hollywood to have them recorded on discs; and that article on the death-throes of Germany which I wrote for *Free World* and which was circulated widely throughout the country by *Reader's Digest* and several big radio stations. Its very title, "The End", betrays its close kinship with the innermost theme of the novel.

Adrian's dialogue with the long-awaited visitor, who in

hidden fashion had long since been introduced, was still in its early stages when a telephone call from my brother Heinrich informed us of the death of her who had shared his life for so many years. The unfortunate woman had made repeated attempts to escape from life by an overdose of sleeping pills. This time she had succeeded. We buried her on December 20 in the cemetery of Santa Monica, and a host of mourners offered their sympathy to the bereaved. He spent the rest of the day with us, and it goes without saying that after the loss he had suffered, our ties became even closer. We made a practice of bringing him to our house with a certain regularity, and also spent many an evening in his place farther out in Beverly Hills, which he chose not to abandon. On such evenings he would read to us from his brilliantly fantastic novel, *Empfang bei der Welt* (*Reception in the World*), as it came into being from his tireless pen. The Moscow *Internationale Literatur* would soon be publishing large parts of his book of memoirs, *Eine Epoche wird besichtigt* (*Sightseeing an Era*). In an essay written for a German journal in Mexico on the occasion of the great writer's seventy-fifth birthday, *Bericht über meinen Bruder*, I attempted to express my admiration for this unique book, for its proud modesty, its futuristic style, compounded of simplicity and leaping intellectualism, and also for its nobly naïve eccentricity. . . .

The ways of life. . . . Ten days after the funeral there was a double baptism: Tonio, the second son of our youngest son, and Dominica, the second daughter of our youngest daughter, Elisabeth Borgese, were consecrated Christians in the Unitarian Church with a minimum of religious ostentation. The ritual struck me as extremely sensible and humane. It was the pleasantest experience I have ever had in church. In the family circle, with Borgese, and also with friends like the Neumanns, we talked again and again of the military situation. Looking back at it now, the range of views that were still possible at the time seems strange indeed. In spite of the desperate situation of Hitler Germany, various possibilities seemed not out of the question —such as indefinite dragging out of the war, with this or that government undergoing changes in the meanwhile, deaths among the leaders, and only after a period of chaos peace concluded by other men. It it was possible to judge the morale of American troops by the mood at home, the situation was not good. Within the country there was hatred for the Jews, the Russians, the English—for everyone except the Germans who had to be fought. The Alliance was constantly endangered from within; what held it together was solely the vigorous diplomacy of Eisenhower, whose landing in Normandy had been an unprecedented masterpiece of strategy. Eisenhower was the faithful executor of the higher will and brilliance of a statesman. But that statesman, lord of the White House for the fourth time, the patrician friend of the people, a match for the European dictators in his cleverness at manipulating the masses, the dictators' born antagonist, the great politician of the good, for whom the popular war against Japan had been a means to strike at the Fascism saved by Munich in 1938—this man was marked by death.

The year ended amid a number of very real political anxieties. The Rundstedt offensive, a last bold act of desperation and a well-prepared attempt by the Nazis to alter the course of destiny, was in full swing and was having alarming success. For a long time now we had been seeing the phrase "withdrawal to more favourable positions" only in the enemy's communiqués. Now it was our turn in eastern France. Loss of all bridgeheads on a fifty-mile front, only the region around Aachen and a strip of the Saar still held, Strasbourg and even Paris itself threatened, panic throughout Europe over the sudden German come-back—such was the picture. It was horrifying to think of the unfortunate Belgians who were once again falling into German hands.

But the adventure petered out. It was a matter of a few days only, and then my daily notes, like the newspapers, were able to ignore it. During those depressing days I had gone on working on the current chapter, and at a gathering in our house shortly after the middle of January I read aloud at one stretch almost all that I had written of the central dialogue—some thirty pages or so. Erika was present and was immediately able to suggest cuts that lightened the text considerably. "Length," I noted, "is the aesthetic peril of this chapter that begins so vigorously—as it is of the whole book. If excitement is to be maintained, given such dimensions, it must be powerful in character."

By the beginning of February the end of the monster dialogue was in sight. With the hysterical declamations of the German radio announcer about the "holy struggle for freedom against the soulless hordes" ringing in my ears, I wrote the pages on hell, which are probably the most powerful thing in the chapter. Inconceivable, incidentally, without the psychological experience of Gestapo cellars. This was the section I brought out for reading aloud again and again, whenever I wanted to present the raisins in the cake for the ends of encouraging self-deception—in other words, the most effective part of the book and one that made my listeners wonder why I was worried about the work as a whole.

It was, I noted, February 20 when I finished the dialogue and felt relieved that it was done. It comprised fifty-two pages of manuscript. Only now was half the book really written, exactly half by page count. It was now all right to permit an interruption, and the very next day I began working out the lecture for Washington which I had already outlined: *Germany and the Germans*. The writing of this took up the next four weeks. By this time the dissolution and putrefaction of the Third Reich was far advanced. Memel had been taken, Posen and Breslau encircled. Refugees were streaming to Berlin and were being driven further on. The *Kölnische Zeitung*, evidently no longer hampered by censorship, frankly reported that panic had seized the Reich from one end of the country to the other. The energies of the people, the army, and the leader had been totally exhausted by five years of war. The Russians, massing their infantry and heavy artillery thirty miles from Berlin, had issued a new appeal to the Germans to eliminate the present régime and surrender, for otherwise national disaster was inevitable. But who was to do the eliminating, who the surrendering? The Nazis had seen to it that the body of the Reich would not be saved alive, that it would have to be carved up piece by piece. Their idea was, we heard in mid-February, to set up a line of resistance in the Austro-Bavarian Alps, with Berchtesgaden as the central fortress, and to retreat there once Berlin had fallen. But rumours of this plan soon faded.

The Big Three manifesto from Yalta announced no abatement of the demand for unconditional surrender. But it expressly said that the Allies had no intention of annihilating the German people. Hitler's troops had completed their retreat to the eastern bank of the Rhine, destroying all the bridges except one, which in mysterious fashion was preserved. It had been expected that the American forces would have great difficulty crossing the river. Suddenly, at the beginning of March, the crossing was effected, the supply lines assured, Bonn taken. During this period I was reading a great deal of Heine, the essays on German philosophy and literature, and his piece on the Faust legend as well. In working on the lecture I remained inwardly close to my principal task and occasionally read aloud from recently finished sections. Social encounters, such as that with Schnabel, Schönberg, and Klemperer at young Reinhardt's house, where after dinner a long discussion of music ensued, likewise helped to preserve contact. While I was writing the passage in the lecture about German romanticism, I read Friedrich Hebbel's diaries and found in them the great sentence (noted down in Paris): "Previous history has only grasped the idea of eternal justice; the future will have to apply it."

An unusually gratifying letter, written by an American soldier in the Philippines, reached me at this time. "I envy you your swift, sure maturity, your heritage of culture, your relentless self-discipline. Such things are hard-won in European civilization. Here in America they are almost non-existent." It made me feel good not only for myself but also for the sake of unhappy and humbled Europe. Certainly this young Yankee did not seem to be an adherent of the "American century". Another American remark also touched me. It was made by our old friend and neighbour, Professor emeritus of philosophy Dean Henry Reiber. Troubled by the melancholy of my article "The End", which had been published in *Free World*, he said to me, pressing my hand: "Don't take the world too hard! Every evening we pray for you."

How differently the patriotic exiles conducted themselves towards my way of feeling and discussing the collapse of Germany! No sooner had I finished writing *Germany and the Germans*, an interpretation of the German tragedy which in our old homeland was to win back many hearts totally alienated from me—than there began a series of rude attacks on my sentiments and my attitude. The barrage was initiated by a Professor von Hentig, writing in the New York Social Democratic newspaper *Volkszeitung*. It was followed by still cruder pens, unfortunately aided and abetted by Alfred Döblin. During the following months the stir flared up again and again, wounding me and depressing me far more than I should have allowed it to.

Preparations for going ahead with *Faustus* were resumed during the latter third of March. I drew up a chronological table and survey of the events and mental processes that were to take place from 1913 to the end, and revised certain items for the book which I had had tucked into my journal, concerning the end of the First World War. I corrected typewritten copies and was not happy. The rush of events in Germany that followed hard upon the crossing of the Rhine and the forcing of the Oder proved to be a serious distraction, without lifting my spirits. "Victorious but hopeless" is the phrase I find in my journal; I seem to have disbelieved in the capacity of the victors to win the peace after the war. A conversation with two Swiss who called on me, a consul and a journalist, revolved around nothing but the conflicts between America and Russia and the impending reconstruction of Germany. "The victory will be squandered worse than last time." Among friends the talk was actually of the "future war of annihilation, which is already a virtual certainty".

"Occupied with the novel. Attempting to find the connection and revive my pleasure in it. Am troubled by dissatisfaction and vexation. I rather think there is no longer any doubt that the work is a failure. Nevertheless, I am going to finish it." I had begun to write Chapter XXVI, the part of the book leading up to the outbreak of the war of 1914. One afternoon—it was the twelfth of April—I picked up the evening newspaper from the end of the driveway, where the carrier usually left it. I threw a glance at the huge headline, hesitated, then mutely handed the newspaper to my wife. Roosevelt was dead. We stood distracted, feeling that the world all around us was holding its breath.

The telephone rang, a request for an extempore radio statement. I refused. We worked out a telegram to the widow of the deceased president, and listened to the radio all evening, deeply moved by the tributes and the mourning from all over the world. During the next several days we cared to hear and read only about him, the details of his death, the funeral in Hyde Park. The shock, the consciousness of a fateful loss, circled the globe. All of us echoed in our hearts the words of noble Eleanor Roosevelt: "I am sadder for our people and for humanity than for ourselves."

And yet there could be no doubt that in America a good many feelings of satisfaction and relief were mingled with the sorrow, were barely concealed behind the official mourning. One can always feel the "whew, that's over!" which greets the death of a great man who has lifted his nation far above its everyday level, for any nation finds that sort of thing strenuous. On this occasion, too, it was not to be missed. We heard of people who had opened bottles of champagne upon hearing the news of Roosevelt's death.

There were many assurances that everything would remain the same as before. The date for the opening of the Allied conference at San Francisco, which the late president had planned to attend, remained unchanged. The war went on. In his address to Congress, Roosevelt's successor held firm on unconditional surrender and the establishment of a lasting peace afterwards. No changes in military operations

D

were in prospect. But the probability was that there would be all the more changes in civilian life. I noted: "An era is ending. The America to which we came will no longer exist."

I took part in the memorial service in the Santa Monica Municipal Building. It was conducted by clergy, a bishop and a rabbi dividing the speaking. In fact, the principal sermon fell to the latter. He formed it into a strange, primordial lament, a kind of desert chant, to which the Jewish group in the auditorium responded, every time the name of the deceased was mentioned, with ritual weeping. My own In Memoriam followed. We were unable to hear the bishop's address, since the English and German texts of my obituary had to be taken to the telegraph office at once. *Free World* and *Aufbau* published it, and it also appeared in Spanish. I made it the basis of one of my last radio broadcasts to Germany, where the newspapers had wallowed in the chance to fling filth at the great adversary of their masters. I had also to prepare a talk to be given at the dinner inaugurating the Interdependence Movement, which had been founded by the philosopher Will Durant. The affair took place on April 22 at the Hotel Roosevelt in Hollywood. Theodore Dreiser was present. Meanwhile, the American general who had captured Weimar made the German civilian population file past the crematoria of the concentration camp there, and informed these citizens, who claimed that they had known nothing, of their share in the responsibility for the horrors that had taken place there in secret and were now exposed to the world. What was found there and elsewhere surpassed in frightfulness all expectation and all conception. Parliamentary committees departed for Germany in order to be able to report on the incredible truth to their San Francisco delegates. We, who had early understood the nature of what in Germany was called "the National State", found nothing surprising and nothing incredible. But the excitement throughout the country, and among us, was enormous. A German woman of our acquaintance, married to an American scholar, felt such shame that for days she refused to show herself in society, and scarcely dared to go out on the street. The Office of War Information requested a statement from me, and I obeyed with an article, *The Camps*, which as the office later informed me received a tremendous distribution.

Events came thick and fast now, a daily hail of fantastic reports: Mussolini captured and put miserably to death; Berlin entirely in Russian hands, the Soviet flag flying from the dome of the Reichstag; more and more suicides among the Nazi bigwigs, who now bit into their providently distributed capsules of cyanide; Hitler and Goebbels dead and burned, and the British press quoting: "The day is ours, the bloody dog is dead." Amid all this I had, to use the expression of my journal, "shouldered" the novel again and was writing—"fluently", in fact—Chapter XXVI, Adrian's installation at Pfeiffering. I even did so on the seventeenth day of May, whose entry reads: "Capitulation of Germany declared. Unconditional surrender signed with appeal to the generosity of the victors. . . . Is this now the day, corresponding with that of twelve years ago, when I began this series of daily notes—a day of fulfilment and of triumph? What I feel is not exactly high spirits. This and that will happen to Germany—but nothing *in* Germany. The malice of a certain group of my fellow countrymen here, the insults they hurl at me because of this conviction of mine, add their bit to overcoming any joy I might feel. There is satisfaction in the sheer physical survival. After the fall of France five years ago, Goebbels had it reported that I was dead. He could not conceive of any other possibility. And if I had taken Hitler's sham victory seriously, if I had taken it to heart, there would in truth have been nothing left for me to do but to pass away. Surviving means victory. By continuing to live I had fought and cast mockery and a curse into the faces of those blasphemers of humanity. So that this is a personal victory of mine, as well. There is no doubt in my mind to whom we are indebted for this victory. It is Roosevelt."

Even during this time I steadfastly maintained my inveterate habit of barring out all outside impressions during the morning hours from nine to twelve or half past twelve, of reserving these hours wholly, as a matter of principle, for solitude and work. Had it not been for this habit, I should scarcely have brought myself to continue, in spite of so many pressures from outside, to write away at Adrian's compositions for poems of Keats and Klopstock (in Chapter XXVII). I proceeded with considerable assistance from Adorno, whose interest in the book grew the more he learned about it and who was beginning to mobilize his musical imagination in its behalf.

The first direct reports from occupied Germany were now arriving. We learned how many persons there had after all, at tremendous risk to themselves, avidly listened to the British radio and to my broadcasts also. Klaus was in Munich as a special correspondent for the *Stars and Stripes*. The outer structure of our house, repeatedly struck by bombs, still stood; the inside, which even before had undergone a good many changes, was altogether destroyed. We knew that under the Nazis it had served for a time as a home for unwed mothers, bearing the name "Spring of Life, Inc." Now an assortment of refugees and bombed-out persons were living in the ruins. It was and remains significant that not a single person who in the early days of the Third Reich attended the auction of our furniture, books, and art objects thought of offering us a single item of the stolen goods. To this day, not one item has ever been returned.

During these May days, a season ordinarily so dear and beneficial to me, there begin to be notes in the journal concerning visits to X-ray laboratories, medical check-ups, blood samples, examination of individual organs of my body—all, incidentally, with reassuringly negative results. Nevertheless, I felt not at all well. The turbulence and shocking phantasms of events in the outer world, the ups and downs of my work, the struggle with the book which meant so much to me, which affected me so deeply, and in which I was pressing forward—all these things placed somewhat too great demands upon my ordinarily obliging constitution. "Everyone tells me that I have grown thinner. Arsenates and vitamins do not stem this continuing slight loss of weight. If only I felt less weak on my feet! Here and there, even very recently, I have done a few good things, but I can feel myself waning." I am using the word in the mythic lunar sense as in the *Joseph* stories. Actually, my nervous fatigue occasionally bordered on exhaustion. At times on my walk towards the ocean I would sit down by the side of the road and be thankful when the car came to bring me home. Yet the date for leaving on the trip to the East was approaching. My seventieth birthday would occur on that trip, and in spite of all the care that I might take I anticipated a varied and demanding time of it.

I set out on the twenty-fourth of the month, together with my loyal wife, supported as I have always been, beyond all gratitude I can express, by her unwavering, loving care. I put my trust in the reserves of strength which are usually released by such enterprises, in the benefits of a change of air and a type of life directed entirely outward. I hoped that my burdens would feel lighter as a result of this interim of uncomplicated celebration of life, which moreover had the further object of fulfilling mighty moral obligations.

X

Travelling was still marked by wartime inconveniences— the train excessively long; the walk from the compartment to the diner a veritable tramp; the standing in line there for a meal sometimes an hour-long test of patience, intensified when close to the goal, by the unpleasant warmth of the kitchen vapours. An elderly gentleman in front of me, hands clinging to the brass pole of the window, drooped in a faint. The military police on the train came to his aid and quickly brought him to where we all longed to be: a table in the dining car. The temptation was strong to follow his example. If only it were easy to faint! My sisters, in their teens, always managed an authentic faint whenever they had no desire to go to church.

En route I read *L'Histoire des Treize*, with mixed feelings as always in the case of Balzac—often carried away by his grandeur, often irritated by social criticism of reactionary hue, Catholic swoonings, romantic sentimentality, and strident exaggeration. We stopped off for a day in Chicago, to visit our children there, and I tried out the Germany lecture on them. It proved to be still too long. I worked it over in the train to Washington, along with Erika, who so often showed herself an artist in omission and contraction, a skilled parer down of all pedantic excess.

In the capital, once again guests in the house on Crescent Place, we enjoyed pleasant holidays. The lecture in the Library of Congress took place before a double audience as usual, one to which I spoke personally and one in the adjoining hall, which heard me over the loudspeaker. It went off nicely. MacLeish, just back from San Francisco, introduced me. His successor as Librarian of Congress, Luther Evans, recommended that the lecture be distributed in Europe by the O.W.I. The reception afterwards in the Meyers' home once again brought a meeting with Francis Biddle, who, if I am not mistaken, had already resigned from his post as Attorney General, and with his wife. Sage Walter Lippmann was also present; my rejection of the myth of a "good" and a "bad" Germany, and my explanation that the bad was at the same time also the good, the good gone astray and in a condition of doom, greatly appealed to him. Antonio Borgese had come from Chicago, Gottfried Bermann Fischer from New York. With the latter there were various items to discuss concerning the new edition of my works which was coming out in Stockholm. Next day I went to visit the Library. I was shown through both buildings, and for the first time obtained some conception of the prodigiousness of this collection which receives everything, includes everything. Dr. Evans produced the actual manuscripts of Johann Cónrad Beissel, the singing master of Ephrata, for even these were faithfully preserved here as curiosities. There they were, spread out on a table before me, and I saw with my own almost incredulous eyes the actual productions of this naïve and dogmatic innovator in music whom I had used so slyly in my novel.

Along with our hosts we were invited to a dinner given by the columnist Drew Pearson. Sumner Welles was present. He spoke with great reasonableness about the future of Germany. What he would recommend was the division of Prussia, a federalist solution in general, and very moderate rectifications of the borders in the East. His programme seemed to me persuasive, humane, and desirable. Actual events, however, were as usual to proceed along an inprudent and foolish path.

We spent one memorable morning in the National Gallery, among the Rembrandts and Italian masters, guided by the director, Mr. David E. Findley, who once we were back in his office presented us with the collections' magnificently illustrated catalogue. I later breakfasted with Elmer Davis and his assistant in the nearby Social Security Building. Here, too, the talk circled around the German question, in connection with my lecture, and I recall the sceptical smiles with which I was met when I told these gentlemen that the notorious "Deutschland, Deutschland über alles" had actually been a very well-meaning slogan, the expression of democratic hopes for a United Germany, and was never intended to imply that Germany was to dominate "over all", only that, once she was united and free, Germans must value her above all sectional interests. Davis evidently took my statements as a patriotic alibi, and we proceded to a highly interesting discussion of the original revolutionary link between the idea of nationalism and democratic freedom. We spoke of the struggle, reactionary but intellectually far from contemptible, of Metternich and Friedrich Gentz against this noble-hearted, unifying, but also explosive mixture.

Then, early in June, came New York, and a string of days filled with festive excitement. I could no longer keep count of all the details in my journal, and here too will pass over most of it in silent recollection. But I wish to say that

I was very sorry to have caused any unhappiness to the fraternity of musicians when I spoke at Hunter College on the part played by musicians in Hitler Germany. I can still remember a phone call I made late at night to sorely troubled Adolf Busch, to let him know that the doubts I had expressed against the most German of the arts were only a form of tribute.

After a party organized by the *Die Tribüne*,[1] for which our learned friend Dean Christian Gauss had come down from Princeton, I sat with Paul Tillich and the writer Heinrich Eduard Jacob over wine, and the latter described from a seemingly inextinguishable memory his experiences in a concentration camp. In the course of this he said certain things about the archaic elements at the bottom of the popular psyche which correspond surprisingly with various comments in the early chapters of *Faustus*.

Along with Åke Bonnier and his American wife, we drove out to Bermanns in Old Greenwich, where a numerous company was gathered and good musicians gave a refreshing performance of Schubert's B flat major Trio. There were many friendly meetings and a wealth of good discussion with Erich Kahler. The evening of June 6 we spent with Bruno Walter and a group of close friends. Hubermann was there; after dinner a number of other friends came, and the two masters played Mozart together—a birthday present such as is not offered everyone. I weighed Hubermann's bow in my hand; it struck me as surprisingly heavy. Walter laughed. "Yes," he said, "the lightness is in him, not in the bow!"

A political banquet of the Nation Associates had been set for June 25. With our daughter Monika we spent ten days in the country, at Lake Mohawk, Ulster County,

[1] German-language weekly published in New York in the 1940's.

in the foothills of the Catskills. The stately hotel called Mountain House, built in the Swiss style and run by Quakers, is situated in a parklike landscape of rugged hills, a kind of nature sanctuary in the Victorian taste. No outside automobile is permitted to enter its precincts, which are full of all sorts of outlooks and sprinkled quaintly with an assortment of turrets and little bridges—an old fashioned *Kurort* without the "cure", unless we regard abstention from alcoholic beverages as a sort of cure. It was just the place for a rest, and at this time of year the air was a good deal cooler than sweltering, stuffy New York. Incidentally, the weather was exhausting and oppressive enough here, too; most of the time it thundered from morning to night. I had difficulty working up my speech for the coming dinner, read letters, read Alfred Einstein's *Mozart* in English translation, and once again *Uncle's Dream*, moved by the lovely figure of Sinaida, who is so impressive by virtue of the emotion the author clearly brings to her creation. This reading sprang from a promise to Dial Press in New York that I would write an introduction for an edition of Dostoevsky's shorter novels. There was a reason for my doing this. During this particular phase of my life, under the sign of *Faustus*, I was greatly drawn to Dostoevsky's grotesque, apocalyptic realm of suffering, in contrast with my usual preference for Tolstoy's Homeric, primal strength.

The newspapers were full of the triumphal passage of Eisenhower, the victor of the war in Europe, through the principal cities of the United States. The accounts did not suppress his oft-repeated warning that America must continue to co-operate with Russia. I have little doubt that certain turns in the general's later career have a great deal to do with this nonconformist attitude, and, were it not for that, he would not today be relegated to being president of

Columbia University. Was not the defeat of Germany in alliance with Russia fundamentally an "un-American activity"? It should in truth have called for a Congressional hearing.

Walking around the lake aroused memories of La Chasté, and so established the mental link with the Nietzsche of Sils Maria[2]—and with my book. In the evening the hotel guests were entertained with motion pictures on the terrace and chamber music in the auditorium. We had been barely a week in Mohawk when sad news reached us. Bruno Frank had died. Despite his gravely strained heart, he had managed to survive a bout of pneumonia in the hospital. Then, home again and lying in his bed one afternoon, an assortment of magazines spread on the quilt, one hand under his head, he had imperceptibly passed away in his sleep, with the most peaceful expression, a Sunday child in death as he had been in life, even amid the iniquities of our times. With these tidings in my heart, I would gladly have given myself to silent retrospect upon the thirty-five years of our friendship, years in which we had almost always lived as neighbours and had enjoyed a constant exchange of ideas. So that I cursed the role of the writer which imposes upon him, on such occasions, the necessity for orderly expression, for phrase-making and wordiness. But the New York German weekly *Aufbau* urgently wanted a memorial article. I spent a sultry-hot morning whipping it into shape, and after all was grateful for the opportunity to pay tribute to this good man, happy poet, and loyal friend.

He had been working on a novel about Nicolas Chamfort, a work of his finest maturity, to judge by the beginning. The first chapter was all that he was fated to finish;

[2] In the Engadine, Switzerland, where Nietzsche lived for some time after he left Basle University.

he had contributed this to the volume of the *Neue Rundschau* which had come out on my birthday, and was more or less in my honour; with this issue the already historic periodical of the old S. Fischer Verlag resumed regular publication. I had the issue with me in Mohawk and now and then cast a hesitant glance into the thick forest of eulogies. My son-in-law Borgese is wont to speak of Vitamin P, that is, praise. And it is true that this drug can have a tonic and reviving effect, and even to a sceptical turn of mind can at least provide amusement. We all bear wounds; praise is a soothing if not necessarily healing balm for them. Nevertheless, if I may judge by my own experience, our receptivity for praise stands in no relationship to our vulnerability to mean disdain and spiteful abuse. No matter how stupid such abuse is, no matter how plainly impelled by private rancours, as an expression of hostility it occupies us far more deeply and lastingly than the opposite. Which is very foolish, since enemies are, of course, the necessary concomitant of any robust life, the very proof of its strength. On the other hand, praise is a food that swiftly satiates, swiftly excites repugnance; the erecting of inner defences against it is soon completed, and probably it would be best therefore if we heard neither good nor evil concerning our affairs. But, alas, that too is not possible for one whose life influences the outside world and affects the minds of others in various ways. . . . It can be deemed fortunate if, as was here the case with the most important of the contributions, the person and his works serve only as a more or less incidental pretext for higher and more general observations. To serve as a springboard for insights into cultural criticism and the philosophy of art is more and better than to be flattered; it is honourable and yields objective profit.

Ringing in my ear is a charmingly abashed "Oh, really?" which was the answer to some words spoken in parting when we left Lake Mohawk. Cynthia, sixteen, was spending the holidays, or part of them, with her parents in this quiet, secluded spot—Cynthia, a college girl with an extremely low opinion of this temporary status in life. What it offered her she characterized, with a shrug, as insignificant. Here she was reading an American "classic" called *The Magic Mountain*, and it was very sweet to see her walking around with it, especially when she wore her light red jacket, a piece of clothing she was partial to, and rightly, even though a certain craft may have been involved, for it wonderfully became her lithe figure. To run into the author of her difficult but for that very reason edifying book was no doubt a surprise, might even be called a youthful adventure; and when at an evening musicale her good mother approached us, to bring about a genuine acquaintanceship, she apologetically indicated that Cynthia was very excited. Sure enough, on this occasion the young lady did have extremely cold hands, but later on this symptom disappeared and we had some friendly talks in the social room or on the deck-like balcony running around the building. Had she found out that frail admiration for the difficult and the edifying might receive reassurance from the counter-admiration which is ever evoked by the comeliness of youth and which, at the end, at the last look into brown eyes, even verges upon tenderness? "Oh, really?"

The Nation Dinner at the Waldorf Astoria in New York likewise passed. It was no small affair. Although the cost was twenty-five dollars a plate, the hall was overcrowded—and no wonder, for the list of speakers was impressive. Robert Sherwood acted as toastmaster, for the first and last time, as he assured me and the public. The speakers were Freda Kirchwey, Justice Felix Frankfurter of the Supreme Court, Negrin, William Shirer, and Secretary of the Interior Ickes. As soon as I too had said my piece, I had to leave to go to the Columbia Broadcasting Company's studios in order to repeat it, in an abridged form, before the microphone. The newspapers published editorials on this highly political banquet. Nevertheless, it was not half so important to me as a dinner conducted in German the following day. We had dined somewhere in the city with the Bermanns, Frau Hedwig Fischer, Fritz Landshoff, Martin Gumpert, Erich Kahler, Kadidja Wedekind, and Monika. Joachim Maass came afterwards, and in our living-room at the Hotel St. Regis I read aloud from *Faustus* to these ladies, publishers, writers, and young girls, read the Esmeralda chapter, the incident of the doctors, the beginning of the conversation with the devil, and the picture of hell. If ever I had derived encouragement from such communication, it was this time, and my journal report of the following day rings with the reverberations of a happy evening.

We set out for home. There was another well-arranged celebration in Chicago, which I owed to the university and, personally, to a kind friend, James Frank, the great physicist. On July 4 we reached home again. The Dostoevsky essay had to be done at once. Worn out and suffering from a cold I produced the twenty-four pages in twelve days, and during the last third of the month I was able to turn back to *Faustus*, going over and correcting earlier material first, and then pressing forward.

XI

During this period I was at work on those parts of the novel where the temporal plane is for ever being shifted, so that the downfall of Germany is counterpointed by the catastrophe that draws ever and more balefully closer. I was also pushing forward the fate of the hero and other inhabitants of the book, the Rodde girls, and Schwerdtfeger, the violinist. These chapters, with their blend of tragedy and grotesquerie, attempt to paint the final stage of a society, when it lies open to ridicule, totally at the mercy of intellectuals' picayune conspiracies. The chapters were also to conjure up *accelerando* the feeling of the *end* in every sense. Fundamentally, every word in them guides the mind toward Leverkühn's decisive and representative work, the apocalyptic oratorio. I had just concluded Chapter XXVII with Adrian's voyage into the depths of the ocean and "up among the stars" (a free adaptation of the chapbook) when news came of "the first attack on Japan with bombs in which the forces of the fissioned uranium atom are released". Thousands of people, each assigned one aspect of the problem, had toiled for years and from the sum total of their mental and physical labour, at a cost of two billion dollars, had made the cosmic forces serve the ends of unparalleled destruction. A few days after the blow fell upon Hiroshima, Nagasaki suffered the same fate. It was a political exploitation of the "innards of nature", to use Goethe's phrase—though Goethe had held that it was not man's destiny to penetrate into the "created spirit". I say "political" because the victory over Japan could have been achieved entirely without the uncanny weapon. It had been used only to prevent Russia's participation in this victory—a motive that did not seem to satisfy even the Vatican, since it expressed concern and religious disapproval. The Holy Father's compunctions were shared by many persons, including myself. Yet, it was after all a good thing that America had won the race in physics against Nazi Germany.

In any case, even before the middle of August came Japan's unconditional surrender. Thus, only six days after the Russian declaration of war upon the island empire, the Second World War officially ended. In reality, nothing ended; rather, an inexorable process of social, economic, and cultural change, which had begun throughout the world a generation before, rolled on without any actual interruption, pregnant as ever with fantastic possibilities. And while the world began one of its blind celebrations, with popular rejoicing and banners waving, I had my own little private cares and troubles, which intermingled with my cares and troubles concerning the novel and distracted my mind from these. The Office of War Information had sent to me an open letter by the German writer Walter von Molo, a document that had appeared at the beginning of August in the newspaper *Hessische Post*. It was an urgent appeal to return to Germany and once more take up residence among the people to whom my existence had for so long been an offence and who had not made the slightest protest against the treatment I had received from their rulers. "Come like a good physician. . . ." It sounded all wrong to me, and the diary attempts to thrust aside this unreasonable disturbing element by constant references to "working on the chapter".

There were other calls. Liesl Frank, in her touchingly ungoverned sorrow for the husband she had lost, wanted to pay tribute to his memory in every possible way. She

planned a large public memorial meeting for later, but first
she wanted a more intimate affair of the same sort. And so
we invited some twenty persons, among them the Feuchtwangers and Bruno Walter, to foregather in our living-
room. From my little reading desk I spoke to them, saying
that this was no hour for hanging our heads, but rather one
for rejoicing in the magnificent legacy our departed friend
had left behind. Before me, and holding the hand of my wife,
sat the bereaved woman, tears streaming from her eyes, but
taking the most heartfelt pleasure in my reading of Frank's
charming story, *Die Monduhr* (*The Moon Clock*), then selected poems by him, then some verses written by Fontane
in his old age—verses Frank and I had always loved for
their artful carelessness and often recited by heart to each
other. Strictly speaking, my physical condition was scarcely
up to such an evening. But who would not expend some
vital strength for a dear departed friend!

The summer was unusually beautiful, brilliant without
heat, zestful as it is only here on this coast, where the ocean
breeze refreshes the air day after day. I finished Chapter
XXVIII (the confusion of Baron von Riedesel) in a mere
ten days and began the following one, the marriage of Inez
with Helmut Institutoris. All the while, however, I was
uncomfortably aware that a reply was forthcoming, and a
fairly thorough reply, to von Molo, or rather to Germany
herself. At an evening at Adorno's I was brought together
once more with Hanns Eisler, and there was good deal of
stimulating pertinent conversation: on the guilty conscience
of homophonic music towards counterpoint; on Bach, the
harmonist (so Goethe had dubbed him); on Beethoven's
polyphony, which, it was said, was not natural and "not as
good" as Mozart's. There was also music in the home of a
hospitable Mrs. Wells in Beverly Hills, where the brilliantly

gifted pianist Jakob Gimbel (one of that incomparable and ever-renewed line of Eastern Jewish virtuosi) played Beethoven and Chopin.

Once again we had a visit from the children and grandchildren from San Francisco. "Seeing Frido again—enchanted. . . . Spent the morning with Frido. Laughed tears over his talk, and was distracted. But wrote away at the chapter anyhow, and am after all curious about the outcome." On the evening of August 26, a Sunday, we had guests to the house, and chamber music: Vandenberg, with American friends, played trios by Schubert, Mozart, and Beethoven. Then my wife took me aside and told me that Werfel was dead. Lotte Walter had telephoned. Towards evening, in his study, where he was revising the newest edition of his poems, he started from his desk towards the door and collapsed lifeless, a little blood in the corner of his mouth. We let our little party come to an end without announcing the news, and after the departure of the guests sat together for a long time in deeply moved conversation. Next morning we went to Alma. The Arlts, Neumanns, Walters, Mme Massary, and others were there. Liesl Frank drove up as we arrived. "A wonderful year, don't you think?" she said bitterly. It was apparent that she was slightly offended because this death somewhat detracted from her own sorrow. And is there not a kind of apotheosis in an artist's death? Does it not mark his entry into immortality, so that those who have loved him and are now bereaved do not wish to face the competition of parallel cases?

I had been away at the time of Frank's funeral; we attended that of Werfel, on August 29. It took place in the chapel of the Beverly Hills funeral home. There were magnificent flowers and a great number of mourners, which included many musicians and writers. The widow, Mahler's widow and now Werfel's, was not present. "I never come to these things," this grand woman had said —a remark which in its frankness affected me as so comic that I did not know whether the heaving of my chest before the coffin came from laughter or sobbing. In the adjoining room Lotte Lehmann sang, with Bruno Walter accompanying. Abbé Moenius' commemorative address was long delayed, amid more and more embarrassed preluding of the organ, since at the last moment Alma had insisted on seeing the manuscript and was giving it a vigorous going-over. Moenius did not speak as a representative of the church, but as a friend of the Werfel household. His address, however, adorned with quotations from Dante instead of the Bible, bore all the earmarks of Catholic culture. In spite of all this, I was overwhelmed by the funeral, by what it was as symbol, as idea; and afterwards, outside, as I greeted friends and acquaintances, I read in their expressions their alarm at my appearance.

"Worked long," the note for the next day reads. I was referring to the novel, but the reply to Germany, the letter to the writer who had exhorted me to come back, could no longer be postponed. Finally and with a sigh, I began to work on it. But then, just as it was that time I replied from Zürich to the faculty of Bonn, many things came to the fore, demanding to be expressed; I felt that here was my chance to set these matters forth in substantial and documentary form. To my shame it took me no less than a full week to complete my answer. Actually, I was done with it on the fifth day, but then I read it aloud to check on its effectiveness—and it became apparent that the conclusion needed to be rewritten, in fact the entire second half. One more day was spent on "various unhappy tries", another and still another conclusion; and yet once more I noted: "Actually have done it all once more." But at last it was completed—in humane spirit, so it seemed to me, in a spirit of conciliation and, at the end, of heartening encouragement. Or so I tried to tell myself, although I could predict that across the ocean what would be heard was chiefly the no. The piece was dispatched to Germany, to the *Aufbau* in New York, and to the O.W.I.

"Reread the current chapter. At last making progress on it." An old book had come my way at the time: *Die Sage vom Faust. Volksbücher, Volksbühne, Puppenspiele, Höllenzwang und Zauberbücher* (*The Legend of Faust, Chapbooks, Morality Plays, Puppet Plays, Conjuring Spirits, and Books of Magic*) by J. Scheible, Stuttgart, 1847, published by the editor. It is a compendium of all the variant treatments of the popular theme and of various critical studies of the subject, including, for example, the essay by Görres on the legend of magic, the control of spirits, and the pact with the devil from his *Christliche Mystik*, as well as a highly curious piece from a work published in 1836: *Über Calderons Tragödie vom wundertätigen Magus. Ein Beitrag zum Verständnis der Faustischen Fabel* (*On Calderón's Tragedy of the Miracle-Working Sage. A Contribution Towards Understanding of the Faustian Legend*) by Dr. Karl Rosenkranz. In this, Rosenkranz cites the following statements from some lectures by Franz Baader on religious philosophy: "The true devil must be the utmost extreme of cold. He . . . must be supreme complacency, extreme indifference, self-satisfied negation. It cannot be denied that such fixation upon empty self-assurance, excluding as it does everything outside this possession of self, is perfect nullity, from which all life is banished, save for the most piercing egoism. But this very iciness would have stood in the way of the representation of the diabolic in literature. For in fiction, we cannot have the stripping of all emotionality. There must be some interest on the part of Satan in order that there be action. The expression of that interest takes the form of irony standing above reality. . . ."

This appealed to me strongly, and I found myself looking into the old volume often. In addition, I was again much preoccupied with Adalbert Stifter. I reread his *Hagestolz*, his *Abdias*, his *Kalkstein*, which I found to be "indescribably original and unobtrusively daring". There are such amazing things in him, like the hailstorm and the fire in the *Geschichte vom braunen Mädchen*. The contrast has often been stressed between Stifter's violent suicidal death and the noble gentleness of his writing. What critics have seldom noticed is that behind the tranquil, tender precision of his observation of nature there lurks a tendency to excess, a penchant for natural catastrophe and pathological elements. This comes out alarmingly in, for instance, the unforgettable description of the terrible blizzard in the Bavarian Forest, in the famous drought in *Heidedorf*, and in the stories just mentioned. The girl's affinity with the thunderstorm in *Abdias*, her power to attract lightning, is another of these uncanny elements. Would anything of the sort be found in Gottfried Keller—though a story like *Der Waldsteig* is otherwise so reminiscent of Keller's type of humour? Stifter is one of the most remarkable, secretly one of the boldest and most strangely thrilling storytellers in world literature. There is so much hidden under the surface in him, and critics have done far too little exploring of his depths.

About this time I foolishly took far too much to heart the rambunctious scribbling of one C. Barth in the New York *Neue Deutsche Volkszeitung*. Simultaneously the O.W.I.

sent to me a wrong-headed and provoking article by Frank Theiss from the *Münchner Zeitung*, in which a group called the Inner Emigration set itself up with a great deal of arrogance. Presumably these "exiles within" were a community of intellectuals who had "kept faith with Germany", not "left her in the lurch in her misfortune", not looked upon her fate "from comfortable box seats abroad", but honestly shared in it. They would have honestly shared it even if Hitler had won. Now the armchair had collapsed around the armchair lookers-on, and for this they took great credit for themselves, were lavish with insults towards those who had breathed the cold winds of exile and whose lot had been, for the most part, misery and death. Theiss himself was grossly compromised when an interview from back in 1933 was published, wherein he came out strongly for Hitler. As a result, the Inner Emigration lost their chief. My nerves were upset by various crude vilifications of me in German-American yellow sheets. Exiles who had returned home wrote against me in the German newspapers. My diary confesses: "The attacks, falsifications, and stupidities tire me like hard work."

There were however compensations and some refreshing experiences. A long essay in the *Nouvelles Littéraires*, containing an appreciation of Louise Servicen's extraordinary French translation of *Lotte in Weimar*, and a study of rare subtlety of the book, cheered me more than all these other things grieved me. Erika sent the periodical to me from Mondorf in Luxembourg, together with an account of how she had visited the Nazi chiefs in their hotel-prison, where they were temporarily quartered while awaiting trial. The emotions of the overthrown tyrants when they learned the identity of the American correspondent ran the gamut from savage abhorrence to expressions of regret that they had

not had a good sensible talk with her, "I would have explained everything to her!" Goering had cried out. "The
Mann case was handled all wrong. I would have done differently." What was that? He would of course have offered
us a castle, a million, and each of us a diamond ring, if we
had been willing to join the Third Reich. Go to your doom,
fat and jovial murderer! You at least enjoyed your life,
while your lord and master lived nowhere but in hell.

Almost simultaneously there arrived the impressive
article that Georg Lukasz had published in *Internationale
Literatur* in honour of my seventieth birthday. This Com-
munist who is deeply concerned with the "bourgeois heritage", and who can write fascinatingly and intelligently
about Raabe, Keller, or Fontane, had earlier—in his series
of essays on German literature in the age of imperialism—
discussed me with intelligence and respect. In doing so he
had maintained the capacity, indispensable in a critic, to
distinguish between opinion and being (or action sprung
from being), and to take only the latter, not the former, at
face value. Irrespective of the opinions I had held at the age
of forty, he nevertheless sets me incontrovertibly side by
side with my brother, and says: "Heinrich Mann's *Der
Untertan* and Thomas Mann's *Tod in Venedig* can both be
regarded as great forerunners of that trend towards signalling the danger of a barbarous underworld existing within
modern German civilization as its necessary complement."
What this does is to lay bare prophetically the relationship
between the Venetian novella and *Faustus*. And it is so very
good because the concept of signalling is of the foremost
importance in all literature and all study of literature.
That the writer (and the philosopher also) is a reporting
instrument, seismograph, medium of sensitivity, though
lacking clear knowledge of his organic function and there-

fore quite capable of wrong judgments also—this seems to me the only proper perspective on writing. Certainly this birthday essay, *The Search for the Bourgeois*, was a sociological and psychological portrayal of my life and work grander in scale and manner than anything I have ever yet received, and hence arousing me to honest gratitude— among other things because the critic did not regard my work only in a historical light, but also related it to Germany's future. It is strange, however, that in all such appreciations, no matter how benevolent, by this particular school of criticism, the *Joseph* novel is consistently omitted or side-stepped. That seems to spring from conformity to a faith, from totalitarian teachings: *Joseph* is myth and therefore represents escape and counter-revolution. It is a pity. And perhaps not quite correct. But since the Catholic Church also does not like the book because it implicitly puts Christianity into relation to earlier beliefs, it must remain a work for the humanist community which can freely enjoy sympathy with the humane that nurtures it.

I do not want to give the impression that good news and comfort came to me only from the non-German world. From Rome Klaus wrote of the posters he had seen everywhere in Berlin announcing lectures on *Joseph* and readings from *Lotte in Weimar*. I heard that things of mine were being read now and then over the revived German radio. *Der Ruf*, the camp newspaper of prisoners of war (now being published in Munich), printed kindly words about me and accorded me its confidence. There were defences of me in German newspapers, in retort to Theiss and the others. In short, the negative side was not unanimous, and why should I expect the affirmative side to be so? One must always repeat to oneself the old motto that I read in my youth on a gable in Lübeck: "It is impossible to please everyone." As though what mattered was such pleasing, and not rather the effect which ultimately clarifies, precipitates out of misunderstandings, controversies, embarrassments. To be sure, this clarification is something very close to death, or comes about only after it. Life is pain, and we live only as long as we suffer.

Letters from old friends also began arriving, now that Germany was open again: from Emil Preetorius, from Hans Reisiger, from younger writers like Wilhelm Süskind; but there was nothing from Ernst Bertram, though I inquired after him here and there without being able to learn anything more than half reassuring. There also came letters from persons one had become accustomed to regard as sinister figures, though they had never meant to be so. It was not easy to answer them—such men as Kirchner of the *Frankfurter Zeitung*, and Hans Blunck, one-time president of Hitler's writers' organization, the *Reichsschriftumskammer*. Moreover, a large number of people wrote from Germany complaining to me that the victors were not distinguishing between the sheep and the goats, between the guilty and the guiltless, were morally throwing all Germans into a single tar-barrel. These implored me to use my "enormous influence" to effect an immediate change.

"Occupied with continuance of the novel (outbreak of the war), using old diaries. Worked hard at Chapter XXX. . . . Not well at night: chills, agitation, cold, disturbed sleep, feeling of approaching illness. . . . The English version of the *Letter to Germany* for the London *News Chronicle* . . . . Hours of work over the mail. . . . Kleist's *On the Marionette Theatre*, Frank Harris's book on Shakespeare. Discussed with K. the monstrousness of this year, the volley of shocks including the many deaths: finally the deaths of Béla Bartok, Richard Beer-Hofmann, and Sea-brook, too, who took his own life. It would be no wonder if one were even wearier. But interest in the novel has revived during these past days. Startled by the unnovelistic, strangely real biographical quality of what is after all fiction. . . . Providing far in advance for future chapters, in spite of so many difficulties still to be coped with. Wrote to Walter in New York to let me have my letter on Frido for a while, in view of the character of Nepomuk Schneidewein. . . . Speech for the Frank memorial celebration finished this afternoon."

For yes, it was the turn of that too, a cup, a sacrifice, gladly made and yet again with a private groan at the inexorability of the demand. The meeting took place on September 29 in the Hollywood Play House. The big hall was filled, all of "Germany in California" had foregathered. My brother too, who so rarely goes out, was with us. There were recitations, readings by trained speakers, who nevertheless were defeated by certain peculiarities of the acoustics, so that they were much annoyed by fearful cries of "Louder!" from the people in the seats to the rear. There followed scattered scenes, much too scattered, from the charming comedy, *Tempest in a Teapot*. I spoke last, before the concluding piano piece—spoke with strain, exhaustion, and from the bottom of my heart. It had been affecting; too affecting, was Heinrich's verdict. Liesl Frank called up next day to say that really a gesture like yesterday's must no longer be asked of me, I gave too much of myself, I must make this the very last time. . . . But suppose they were to hold a Franz Werfel memorial?

I was engaged on Chapter XXXI, which describes the end of the war, the devoted women who serve Adrian, and Adrian's turning to puppet opera. "In the evening read the *Gesta Romanorum* for a long time. The loveliest and most surprising of the stories is that concerning the birth of the sainted Pope Gregory. He is marked out for sanctity from birth, being the product of intercourse between brother and sister and then committing incest with his mother—all of which, to be sure, he atones for by an incredible seventeen-year span of asceticism on the solitary rock. Extreme sinfulness, extreme pentinence; this alternation alone creates holiness." I knew nothing of the multitudinous forms the legend had taken, had scarcely heard of Hartmann von Anue's Middle High German poem. But I liked it so well that even at that time I toyed with the thought of stealing the subject from my hero and myself making a little archaic novel of it.

On November 9 I began Chapter XXXII, with the troubling conversation between Inez and Zeitblom, and finished it twenty days later. Preparations were begun at once for the next, which was again to use the device of "double time", carry out the motif of the little sea-maid, and point up for the reader Schwerdtfeger's elusive flirtatiousness. But my state of health, intensified snuffling and coughing, a lasting catarrh, and unwell appearance, once more led me to consult the doctor.

The result corresponded to my own feeling; the doctor found further loss of weight, too low blood pressure, mucous obstruction of the bronchia. He wrote out various prescriptions for bolstering my nutrition. And so back to the novel, equipped with fat red vitamin capsules to swallow three times daily, which I did with great difficulty. With the coming of December, I began working out Chapter XXXIII in a happier frame of mind, since there was nothing seriously wrong and my heart had once again proved to be sound as a bell. Only, it was unfortunate that just now, when the most difficult task of all was looming closer every day—to provide a convincing, precisely realistic description, one of utter versimilitude, of Leverkühn's apocalyptic oratorio, an affair which would take three chapters since I had realized at once that I wanted to intertwine the analysis of this ominous last work with a depiction by the good Serenus (in the arch-fascistic gatherings at Kridwiss') of the whole unhealthy complex of the time—it was unfortunate that just at this point this everlasting tracheal and bronchial catarrh should have so debilitating an effect upon me, sometimes making me well-nigh decrepit. It was likewise unfortunate that I should have to appear at several public meetings. At Royce Hall, Westwood, in the presence of delegates from the Russian consulate, I gave a lecture based on my old Dostoevsky essay. To my delight Klemperer, who was present, took a special part in this affair. And I was asked to be one of the speakers at a dinner given by the Independent Citizens Committee, to which Professors Shapley and Dykstra, Mrs. Helen Gahagan-Douglas of the House of Representatives, and Colonel Carlsson belonged. The high point of the evening was the address by the colonel (later a general, and now no longer living), who courageously lashed out against the misuse of our troops in China, where they had no business to be— the less so since the only part of the country where any order prevailed was the part organized by the Communists. . . . How different, and how interesting in their own fashion, were the evening receptions to which we were occasionally invited by Count Ostheim, a scion of the Hohenzollerns and pretender to the throne of Weimar, who had early been driven into exile because of his anti-militarism and other disqualifying opinions, and his American wife. There we met an international society, scrambled and elegant, and heard aristocratic White Russian exiles tell tales of how the Stalin régime had sought to have them extradited. That might have been true—although I found it hard to believe that Moscow regarded these gentry as dangerous. But, then, what were they doing in the "red prince's" salon? This we must understand. Exile creates a special form of life, and the various reasons for banishment or flight make little difference. Whether the cause is leftism or the opposite—the sharing of a common fate and class solidarity are more fundamental than such nuances of opinion, and people find their way to one another.

"Still at the chapter." "Some work on the chapter." "Nearing the end of XXXIII." Finally, on December 27: "Finished XXXIII! Read it aloud." Perhaps I am after all too critical of the whole, out of weariness. Read the Apocalypse; moved by these words: "You have some small strength and have kept my word and have not denied my Name."

XII

As early as the beginning of December I had taken the resolve, and accomplished it, to hand over to Adorno everything that had so far been written and typed out, in order to give him a complete insight into the unfolding of the novel's ideas, to acquaint him with my intentions, and to cajole him into helping me with the impending musical problems. Towards the end of the year, therefore, I put my morning's work aside one day and wrote Adorno a ten-page letter in which I apologized as best I could for my "scrupulously unscrupulous" borrowings from his philosophy of music. I had done this, I wrote, in the confidence that what I had borrowed, what I had learned, might attain an independent function within the work, a symbolic life of its own, and in so doing remain untouched at its original site. I went on to explain how vital it was for my "tyro's ignorance" to be supplemented by professional knowledge. "The novel," I wrote, "has reached the point at which Leverkühn, at the age of thirty-five, experiencing a first wave of euphoric inspiration, composes in a fantastically short time his chief work, or his first principal work, the *Apocalipsis cum figuris*, based on the fifteen Dürer woodcuts, or else directly on the text of Revelation. The problem is to imagine, realize, graphically describe a work of art (which I regard as a highly German product, as an oratorio with orchestra, choruses, soloists, and a narrator). I am really writing this letter to linger on my problem, which I do not yet quite trust myself to attack directly. What I need are a few concrete details which will help with characterization and contriving a sense of reality (one can make do with little), which will give the reader a plausible, in fact a convincing, picture of the opus. Would you join me in putting your mind to the question: how is the work—I mean Leverkühn's work—to be got underway; and how you would do it if you had a pact with the devil? Could you give me one or two musical ideas to help promote the illusion? What I have vaguely in mind is something satanically religious, diabolically pious, seeming at one and the same time strictly bound by form and criminally irresponsible, frequently a mockery of art itself; and also something that goes back to primitive, elementary levels of music (memories of Kretschmar's Beissel lectures), abandoning the division into bars, even the ordering of notes (trombone glissandi); furthermore, something which could hardly be executed in practice; old church modes, *a cappella* choruses which have to be sung in untempered tuning, so that scarcely a note or an interval occurs on the piano—etc. But 'etc.' is easy to say. . . ."

This matter of the choruses in untempered tuning was a foolish obsession of mine to which I obstinately clung for a long time, although the specialist I had appealed to would not hear of it. I was so in love with the notion that I even consulted Schönberg about it, behind Adorno's back, so to speak. "I would not do it," Schönberg replied to me. "But it is altogether possible theoretically." In spite of being thus empowered by the highest authority, I finally let the idea drop, and instead of having Adrian abandon division into bars, I had him ironically preserve them as a bow to the achievements of civilization. On the other hand I made a great deal of the barbarism of instrumental and vocal glissandi.

Christmas—another rainy one—for the time being. Michael's family from San Francisco—Mill Valley— arrived for the holiday, and since we had no tinsel for the tree, we were busy on Christmas Eve cutting up a quantity of carefully saved tinfoil into narrow strips, to please the boys. "Seeing Frido again—how happy it makes me." I went on with Chapter XXXIII during the holidays, weaving into it Adrian's strangely insistent observations about the beauty and truth of the sea-maid, and completed it shortly before the end of the year. It had cost me twenty-seven days. Adorno sent word that he had read everything and had prepared some notes which we would discuss together. "Tinkering with the chapter. Overwhelmingly tired on my walk, unwell and sleepy the rest of the day, without being able to sleep. Saw Dr. Schiff. (Up to now it had been Doctor Wolf, but repeated changes of doctors is typical of conditions like mine; before it was over, Dr. Rosenthal, my brother's doctor, would also have his turn.) In his opinion the tracheal and bronchial catarrh was probably infectious, and he prescribed all sorts of balms, antiphlegmatics, and tonics." So the diary reads. All very well: I had no fever, was not ill, but only half ill, and therefore clung to my routine, to my accustomed round of work, reading, tramping down to the ocean, dictating letters, and writing others. "Why does everyone who wants to immigrate or is looking for a job appeal to me!" A question to destiny. Preparations for Chapter XXXIV, which was to be divided into three parts, began at once with the new year, 1946; the first day's entry for that year related to *Faustus* as a whole. This was in connection with my looking through Max Osborn's *Memoirs*, the author having asked me for a preface. Reading there about Menzel, Liebermann, Klinger, Lesser-Ury, Bode the lord of museums— reading about these men, I noted: "All sheer personalities! I think I am none. I personally will be as little remembered as Proust." And suddenly: "How much *Faustus* contains of the atmosphere of my life! A radical confession, at bottom. From the very beginning that has been the shattering thing about the book."

One afternoon during the next few days I went to see Adorno. He and his wife had read the manuscript, taking the pages from each other's hands. And I, the doubter, listened avidly to their account of the empathy, suspense, excitement with which they had read. It greatly relieved my conscience to see that the author of the *Philosophy of Modern Music* was so gracious about the way I had provided my devil, who is "against 'works'," with some of his critical *aperçus*. Later on, when I was alone with him in his study, he said a great many good and clever things concerning

124

the grandeur and the difficulty of my project. He was already familiar with much of the manuscript from my readings aloud; much of it had been new to him, and he expatiated particularly on the "humanity" that emerged from the section on the devoted women, and the "experience" implicit in Inez Rodde's passionate revelations to Serenus, the "good soul" who aroused no emotions. Adorno was not very taken with the idea, to which I had long been addicted, of basing the oratorio on Dürer's apocalyptic woodcuts, and we agreed that the interior of the work must be extended as far as possible into the realm of general eschatology, that it must as far as possible include within it the whole "apocalyptic culture" and be made a kind of resumé of all proclamations of the end. I had had something of the sort in mind myself, for the extent to which John of Patmos borrowed from other visionaries and ecstatics is certainly striking. It is curious how there are age-old conventions and traditions of this sort, by means of which the victim of hallucination may draw upon fixed visions and experiences. I was struck, as the text puts it, by the fact "that a raving man should rave in the same pattern as another who came before him; that one is ecstatic not independently, so to speak, but by rote". This psychological item seemed to me extremely interesting and worth stressing, and I thought I knew why. It coincided in a way with my own growing inclination, which as I discovered was not mine alone, to look upon all life as a cultural product taking the form of mythic clichés, and to prefer quotation to independent invention. *Faustus* shows many a trace of this leaning.

Adorno did not yet have any musical instructions and directions for Leverkühn's opus which he could give me, but he assured me that he was thinking about the matter, that he already had all sorts of ideas stirring inside him, and that he would shortly be ready to assist me. Not to relate the way in which he kept his word would be to leave these memoirs very incomplete. During the weeks to come I sat with him many a time with notebook and pencil, over a good home-brewed fruit liqueur, jotting down cue phrases concerning corrections and more exact details for earlier accounts of works of music in the book, as well as traits he had conceived for the oratorio. Fully cognizant as he was of the intentions of the whole and of this particular section, he aimed his suggestions and recommendations precisely at the essential point, namely, to make the opus open simultaneously to the criticism of bloody barbarism and to the criticism of bloodless intellectualism.

The preparations for this decisive section had lasted a long while—I had been reading Dante, studying the Apocrypha and all kinds of essays on apocalyptics and on ancient Christian conceptions of the hereafter, writings which seemed to come my way of their own accord. Towards the middle of January 1946 I began the writing, and it was to claim my energies until the beginning of March, that is, for six weeks. This was not long, for those energies of mine were subject to greater and greater fluctuation. The diary shows an increase in brief comments on headaches, nights of coughing, nervous weakness, and "absurd" fatigue. Yet how many things had to be dashed off in this interval, how many contributions to this and that! I had, for example, to speak at a meeting "in defence of academic freedom", and to dictate a radio address commemorating Roosevelt on his birthday. Within this period I also undertook a task at once dear to my heart and of documentary importance, the writing of the *Bericht über meinen Bruder* (*Report on My Brother*).

There were also cheering impressions to raise my

drooping spirits. Käte Hamburger's book on *Joseph and His Brothers* was published in Göteborg, Sweden. Reading this penetrating commentary by a philologist, I felt a kind of envy for that period in my life when I had played gaily with mythology. The macabre work I was presently engaged on left so little room, none at all in fact, for such games. I found fault with it for being unepic, unhumorous, dreary, artistically unfortunate. And yet a first echo of it was beginning to reach me, the voices of some of the earliest readers of the unfinished manuscript, consoling voices, and more moving when fixed in writing than all the spoken encouragement I had received now and then. Erich Kahler in Princeton was seizing the typewritten manuscript in sections from the translator, Helen Lowe-Porter. He had taken as much as she had of it, and he, who was one day to do the magnificent analysis of the book called *Secularization of the Devil*, now wrote to me about these opening sections in terms that gave me pleasure naturally proportionate to the anxieties and doubts this woeful work aroused in me. The loyal translator herself, for the most part so reticent from sheer modesty before the work entrusted to her, likewise sent a letter. "I strongly feel," she wrote, "that in this book you will have given your utmost to the German people."

What else can we ever do but give our utmost? All art which deserves the name testifies to this determination to reach the ultimate, this resolve to go to the limits; all art bears the sign, the scar, of the utmost. It was this, the feeling of a will to dare the utmost adventure, that fascinated me in Werfel's utopian posthumous novel, *Star of the Unborn*, which I was currently reading. The translator, Gustav Arlt, had let me have the typescript of the original. One chapter in it, the gymnastics of the chronosophic school class in interplanetary space, had appeared in the June issue of the *Neue Rundschau*, contributed by the now deceased writer as a birthday gift for me. It closes with the mystic paradox that a magnitude can exceed itself in magnitude, that the energy of a star can be greater than itself, and that this is the situation in miracle, the love-sacrifice, self-destruction through glorification. The moral poetry of the idea (if it can be called an idea) had stirred me curiously and deeply at the time it was freshly written, and Werfel had told me that he had chosen this chapter for me precisely on this account. I rediscovered something of its transcendence in the whole work, which had been written in a way after the author's death, his heart already shattered, so that it seems a spiritistic work in more senses than one. The book has a coldness which no longer belongs entirely to life and which cannot be called artistically happy. The speech and the psychic life of these men living on earth hundreds of thousands of years after us are both over-spiritualized and overtechnologized; and the picture of them, their speech, their psychic life, has something—I repeat the word—spiritistic about it, empty and hollow. The strangest, most bizarre features are introduced into this infinitely remote age—for example, advertising posters composed of moving stars, or the fact that people no longer move to a destination but use an instrument to bring it to themselves in some technico-spiritual way. Notions of this sort are like dream inspirations: during the dream they seem extremely good and usable, but when you awaken they prove to be sheer nonsense. Here, apparently, no critical awakening took place—there was no longer time for that. And if it were not for the comic elements that are smuggled in, such as the innocently incorrect speech of the dogs who always say "nod" instead of "not", there would be a strong temptation to turn away in boredom from a work which affects one as lifeless. Still, after all, there are absolutely magnificent, absolutely fascinating intuitions in this excessively venturesome narrative of death; there are illogicalities, novelties, products of an already otherworldly and for that very reason brilliant imagination. The at once absurd and disturbing scenes and events in the underworld, inside the hollow space in the earth, with its oppressive, nightmarish atmosphere, have scarcely any match in all literature as imaginative achievements. For me, the strangest attraction, stimulation, and significance of the book consisted precisely in its secret ties with world literature, in the fact that in its discursive fashion it continues a tradition, particularly in its express quality as a travel novel. As such it reminds us, and is itself reminded, of Defoe, also of Swift and Dante. The reminiscences of the latter are most deliberate of all, though not necessarily the happiest, for in contrast to Dante the book has no real language of its own. I read it twice, the second time with pencil in hand, and toyed with the thought of delivering a lecture on it. I never got around to that.

On February 2 Hubermann gave a concert in the Philharmonic Hall at Los Angeles. We did not allow ourselves to be disheartened by the long ride, but went to hear the ugly little wizard who had always had so much of the demonic fiddler about him. He played Beethoven, Bach (a *chaconne* in the course of which he extracted from his violin strange organ effects), a charming sonata by César Franck, and some gypsy-like encores. Afterwards we presented ourselves in the crowded green room to see him. He cried out with delight when he caught sight of us. Our acquaintance and sympathy were of long standing and had often been renewed in Munich, Salzburg, Zürich, The Hague (where we lived together at the German ambassador's) and New York. On the 5th he came to our house for dinner and invited us to his country place above Vevey if, as we planned, we came to Europe. He was dead when we saw Switzerland again.

Another memorable visit was that of Karsh, the great Canadian photographer, he who had made the famous portrait of Churchill with that grimly reflective smile. Churchill had granted him five minutes, and it was his boast that he had taken the Prime Minister's cigar away from him for that period of time. In my case he was able to proceed more deliberately. With an assemblage of apparatus that repeatedly caused short circuits, he worked with me for nearly two hours on a series of takes. Several of these, in their success as likenesses and their graphic lighting effects, represent the utmost in perfection that I have ever seen in photographs, not in just those of myself. It was a pity, though, that at that time I was in such bad form as a model, so that the otherwise splendid portraits show me looking rather uncharacteristically pallid, with peaked features and too much spiritualization.

Photographic experiments of a graver nature, X-rays of my lungs, had brought to light a shadow somewhere in them, and the doctor said that it would be well to keep an eye on it. For the present he recommended treatment of nose and throat by a specialist, Mantschik by name, a Gallicized Pole with a most skilled hand, who did his best to alleviate the symptoms. It was becoming more and more apparent, however, that these symptoms were of a secondary character. I had for some time been having slightly higher temperatures afternoons and evenings, although I only half admitted this to myself. I had another such mild fever the evening of the day I completed the oratorio section. That evening I went with my brother to a recitation given by Ernst Deutsch in the Warner Studio. I had already missed a similar performance by this prominent actor and remarkable speaker and could not this time decline his cordial written invitation. Numerous acquaintances were there, and I enjoyed the evening greatly, in that somewhat faraway, at once weak and elevated, state into which we are cast by a moderate fever. It was late before I went to bed— and for several days thereafter I did not leave it, having come down with a grippy illness that brought about fevers of 102° every afternoon. Penicillin taken orally every three hours day and night had no effect. The empirin-codeine mixture went on being more helpful to me. I slept a great deal, by day also, and read considerably, chiefly Nietzsche, for the lecture on him seemed to be the most pressing item on my programme of work. In the following days I seemed to recuperate, but there remained a tendency for relapses into fever. Some of this time I spent out of bed, or in bed only in the mornings, reading and dozing. A crisis had risen in the United Nations over Iran and over the Anglo-American military alliance instituted by Churchill. It led to a duel of words between Churchill and Stalin. Churchill spoke with polish and Stalin coarsely; neither, I felt, was altogether wrong. This is generally my reaction, and there is only one instance in my life—and this is significant—when I have not had it. Hitler had the great merit of producing a simplification of the emotions, of calling forth a wholly unequivocal No, a clear and deadly hatred. The years of struggle against him had been morally a good era.

A spell of semi-recuperation and relapses into fevers followed. I drove out and walked somewhat, but it did me no good; in particular, the sea breeze, which I ordinarily loved, was harmful to me. I saw guests for tea, but afterwards my wife, shaking her head, would bring down the thermometer, which had been left upstairs, and when it showed more than 98·6 would send me off to bed. I went over much of Nietzsche again, especially the writings of the early seventies and his *Use and Disadvantage of History*, and took notes. We celebrated my brother's seventy-fifth birthday with a small party, and I recall an interesting conversation with him on the subject of my lecture. At his urging, I put myself under the care of Dr. Friedrich Rosenthal. He gave me injections of my own blood, which proved fruitless, and then tried an empirin-bellergal cure, to suppress the fever. In the meantime he had sent for the latest X-ray photographs of the lung, and would have it that they clearly showed infiltration of the right lower lobe. He insisted on consulting a specialist, an American, who confirmed the finding and suggested that the existence of the abscess be definitely established by bronchoscopic examination. He also hinted at the necessity for an operation.

I was more surprised than alarmed, for I had never thought that danger would ever threaten me from my organs of respiration; the doctors, moreover, agreed that the trouble was not tubercular in character. "Much about my state of health during recent months is explained by this discovery," I wrote. "Under what unfavourable circumstances I have worked! On the other hand, the terrible novel together with the vexations over Germany are certainly responsible for this illness, which the *grippe* has only activated. . . . Postponement of the lecture series until October definitely decided."

Here the diary breaks off.

XIII

The vigorous fashion in which matters henceforth proceeded, and fortunately so, was due solely to my wife, the only one of us who knew what she wanted and who took the necessary steps. Dr. Rosenthal was at bottom against the operation on account of my age; in fact, to spare me, he was also against the bronchoscopy, concerning which the American doctor had genially remarked that I would recover from in a week's time. Dr. Rosenthal, out of sheer humanity, was not disinclined to wait, depending on my basically sound organism to resorb the abscess without an operation. One argument in favour of this course was the success of a penicillin injection cure; a nurse had been brought in to administer this eight times in twenty-four hours. The drug completely eliminated the fever, and from then on I never had it again. Nevertheless, we all know that this method of letting nature take its course involved considerable risk. While the doctor hesitated and I myself found it easiest to let others decide what was to be done with me, my wife had made up her mind. She got in touch with our daughter Elisabeth Borgese in Chicago, and Elisabeth in turn with the university's Billings Hospital. Here one of the foremost surgeons in America, Dr. William Elias Adams, works; he is especially noted as a pneumotomist. Arrangements were quickly made at that end; railroad reservations and ambulance transportation to the station were provided for at this, and before I knew it I found myself outside our front door, under the troubled eyes of our Japanese couple, Vattaru and Koto, for I was lying on a stretcher which was slid into an ambulance.

In such novel circumstances I was driven swiftly and

gently to Union Station, where arrangements had been
made for me to be carried straight to our own bedroom on
the train. There, reclining on the bed in my bathrobe, I
spent the next thirty-six hours, while my wife sat by in
utter discomfort. Elisabeth was waiting for us in Chicago,
and once more an ambulance stood ready. On the wheeled
stretcher I was taken up in the elevator, down the broad
corridors of Billings Hospital, and into the room made
ready for me, which the dear child had already decorated
with flowers. How vividly I can still see this whole arrival
and installation—I who had never had a taste of the routine
of a large hospital, had never had anything to do with surgery. I can recall every item of those first hours—how I
made the acquaintance of the pendulum clock suspended on
the wall, how the nurses floated back and forth, taking
temperatures, giving injections, dispensing soothing tab-
lets; how the doctors who were to treat me came *in corpore*
to pay me a welcoming visit, at their head the surgeon himself. Dr. Adams was a man of unpretentious amiability and
kindliness, without a trace of the tyrannical habits of the
German-type institutional despot before whom assistants
and nurses trembled. He had with him his medical adviser,
specialist in internal medicine and university professor, Dr.
Bloch—tall, brown-haired, born in Fürth near Nuremberg, as he soon confided to me in German. There was
also Dr. Phillips, a lung specialist, with a turn for jest and
easy chatter; Dr. Carlson, the intern, only twenty-four, of
Scandinavian descent and handsome as they come, a young
man distinguished by outstanding intelligence and manual
skill—and a considerable white-jacketed entourage in addition. These were pleasant personal impressions for the
beginning.

Afterwards, Professor Bloch exerted his authority to

take over the general examination from the assistant, who had already begun it. His interrogation on the prehistory of the illness was friendly and precise. Incidentally, it was written down later by younger assistants, my wife dictating the case history for hours. Formally speaking, the decision for operation had not yet been made; it was still dependent upon the result of the bronchoscopy, although that result could be fairly well anticipated.

This procedure formed one of the most striking events of the next ten days, during which time I became familiar with my ingeniously constructed hospital bed, which could be cranked to whatever height I wished at head and foot, and with the mode of life of patients in general—with the institutional day, which began early and ended early. Once again extended on a stretcher and pushed into the elevator, I was transported to lower floors, where a cluster of familiar faces were assembled, having come either to take part directly in the exploratory act, or to look on. Among them was Friend Bloch. The delicacy and consideration of the procedure came as a surprise to me; the methods were magical, and I was enormously grateful. For a start my throat was swabbed with some anaesthetic solution. Then, while my head lay in an assistant's lap (later, I suppose, he would have to raise it quickly), a white-smocked woman of the active, energetic type gave me an injection in the crook of my left arm, telling me that I would soon become sleepy. Sleepy? I had spoken scarcely two words when consciousness vanished gently and utterly, and—probably only for a short time, five or six minutes—I was profoundly unaware of anything that was happening to me. What did happen must be quite painful to accept with the mind awake—the California consultant had said, after all, that it would take me a week to recover from it. Here there was no necessity for recovery because I had undergone no strain. I awoke, back in my room, to find good Dr. Adams, who had accompanied me there, mercifully helping me to blow my nose. For to have an apparatus equipped with a tiny electric light introduced down the trachea into the lung (a kind of periscopic arrangement permitting the physician to see exactly how things are in those parts) naturally causes irritation of the entire respiratory tract. There is mucus and a small amount of blood to be brought up, and after being returned to your bed you need a few paper handkerchiefs. But that is the extent of the discomfort. I was delighted, and for days afterwards, to the amusement of the young doctors in particular, I spoke with admiration, praise, and gratitude of the magical injection.

The narcotic, which has not been in use for very long, is called pentothal, if I am not mistaken, but I never heard the name so long as I was in the hospital. Among the curious laws and reticences of these places is the fact that you never find out what is being done for you, and you soon learn to feel that curious inquiries are tactless. The nurses refuse to tell you anything about your temperature chart. They will never betray the constituents of the white lozenges that they serve in a glass of water every few hours. Neither will a doctor divulge the name and nature of a medicament he has prescribed. I recall how, during my convalescence, my digestion was slightly upset by some baked fish. Late in the evening I asked for the intern who happened to be on duty, to tell him my trouble. In such cases, I said, I had always resorted to half a teaspoon of bicarbonate of soda. He ignored that. For some time he continued to inquire about the symptoms of the disorder and the possible cause. Finally he said: "Well, don't worry, we will give you a little something which will be helpful." The nurse brought the "little something" in a cup. It was bicarbonate of soda.

The operation had now finally been decided on. In the absence of Dr. Adams, who had left for a medical conference, the next five or six days were spent in every imaginable preparation and precaution. Blood samples, expeditions via wheel chair or stretcher to the X-ray laboratory, visits from various specialists of the hospital came in rapid succession. As far as my heart was concerned, in particular, the doctor—English, if I remember rightly—was very well satisfied. With that heart, he declared, I could stand any kind of operation.

A highly important personage likewise called—Dr. Livingstone, wife of my surgeon and mistress of the art of anaesthesia, canny compounder of narcotizing fluids. I made her promise that in the main operation I would once again experience the blessings of that glorious injection in my arm.

The time came for establishment of the pneumothorax, that is to say, the introduction of nitrogen into the thoracic cavity in order to stop the activity of the diseased lung. And it was after all curious to experience, upon my own body, a technique of which I had so often spoken in bygone days, when I was working on *The Magic Mountain*. Professor Bloch undertook this, with great accuracy and skill, and young Carlson watched with intense eagerness to learn. The whole business could scarcely be called discommoding, but Bloch praised me warmly for my co-operativeness, and when I expressed surprise, he said: "You have no idea what a fuss people often make about it."

Meanwhile Erika, at the news of what was happening, had flown through the ether from Nuremberg to join us and stand by her mother, who was staying at the Borgeses' and spending the greater part of the day at my bedside. Nothing could have been more comforting and welcome to both of us than the presence of this sprightly and loving child of ours, who always enlivens things for us. She made it her business to take care of the flowers with which my room had filled—laurels, as it were, issued before the battle, but a pleasure to the eyes, and I doted on them with as much pride as any other inhabitant of the crankable beds—"just another patient", as one of the nurses had described me to acquaintances who asked after me. I had neither fever nor pain, but was so weak that even shaving meant excessive exertion. Consequently, the blood transfusion that I received a day or two before the operation was probably not entirely superfluous. Two young interns carried it out according to regulation, and while the preserved blood trickled slowly into my veins I entertained the two by reading one of those amazing news-sheets that Erika used to fabricate by pasting together words and phrases from newspapers: "4-Power Showdown Triumph Bulletin 1946, Released after Wild Ride for Germany," with such headlines as "Truman Sniffs at U.S. Policy," "Eisenhower May Be Arrested on Spy Charges," "Germany Demands Dismissal of U.S. Government. Explains Why," "Russia Asked to Neglect Red Defence," "Truman Hopes to Lure Stalin to Missouri, Pepper Says," "Foreign-Born Babies by War, Navy Leaders Pose Problem—Ike Will Recognize Quintuplets—Bradley Favours Murders," and so on and so forth. . . . In consequence, a somewhat improper hilarity prevailed during the transfusion, but I wanted to see these young people laugh because it made it easier for me to master the slight horror I had of the business.

Then Adams was back and declared that, if I had no objection, we could go ahead. Tomorrow morning it was to be, then. My wife insisted, in slight violation of hospital rules, on spending the night in the dreadfully uncomfortable armchair beside my bed, while I slept the sleep of perfect peace of mind. Nevertheless, in the afternoon I had asked Dr. Bloch what the word for *lampenfieber* was in English. "Stage fright," he had replied. On the dot of seven o'clock, as usual, the day began with the morning toilet. I received my hypo (it was morphine, of course, but who would have dared to ask) and then, from the stretcher that carried me away, I waved good-bye to my faithful dear ones, who were remaining behind. I shall never forget the gentle atmosphere in the semi-dark ante-room to the operating room, where I had to wait awhile on my stretcher. People moved around me, but they walked on tiptoe, and those who came up to me for a brief greeting did so with the greatest delicacy. Bloch thrust his head through the door and nodded to me. "No stage fright today," I informed him, but he did not enter into my joke. Dr. Adams bade me good morning and informed me that in addition to my beloved injection I would be given a little something to inhale. I was touched by his conscientiousness. "Well do I know Ireland's Queen," I quoted to myself from *Tristan and Isolde*, meaning Dr. Livingstone. This lady promptly sat down beside me and first busied herself with my arm (perhaps she only pretended; for what does a little pentothal amount to when protracted work is in prospect?). Then, with a gentle hand, she placed the mask soaked in noble essence upon my face. Gone. It was the most peaceful, unfrightening, and swiftest anaesthesia imaginable. I think it took but a single breath to transport me into the most utter absence—though during the next one and a half or two hours more had to be trickled on at frequent intervals. I had no part in that, so far as I knew, but from all I heard later, they were smiling hours. It was a beautiful morning; everyone had slept so splendidly that they were all hale and in good spirits, first of all Dr. Adams, who worked with his accustomed mastery, never hurrying, the tempo precisely calculated, but saving time nevertheless by the precision of each stroke. His task was eased, moreover, by the sound constitution of his patient (I needed only one transfusion during the operation where other, younger, people need two or three). That, combined with advanced medical technique, produced an almost sensational clinical success. For days afterwards, I heard, medical circles in New York and Chicago discussed this "most elegant operation".

My wife, Erika, and Medi spent the hours of suspense in Dr. Bloch's office. From time to time he came in to report to them. "It is going well; it is going very well," he said, but his hand was cold. Later my wife was by my bedside when, long since restored to my room, I temporarily awoke. Still very dazed, I spoke to her in English, which is not at all my habit. And strangely enough, I complained. "It was much worse than I thought," I said. "I suffered too much!" To this day I ponder upon the significance of this nonsense. What was I talking about? For I had felt none of it, after all. Do there exist some vital depths in which, with all the senses shut off, one nevertheless suffers? Is suffering inseparable from enduring in the lowest depths? This thought might even apply to the so-called dead organism. No one knows how dead it is before its actual dissolution; that fact might serve, if only as a wary question, as an argument against cremation. To put it in English once more: "It may hurt."

The after-effects of the anaesthesia were minor; they scarcely bothered me as I slept on and on. I was given some warm water, and cold water too as a change, to drink through a glass tube. The loss of fluids in such an operation is considerable. Around seven o'clock I asked the doctor making the rounds what time it was. He told me. "You're up early," I said in surprise. "Not quite," he replied. "It is still the same day." Already I was asleep again. I think it was that same night, or early in the morning, that I was given orange juice through the glass tube. Never in my life has anything tasted so wonderful to me. It was ecstasy. Apparently thirst and hunger were equally satisfied by this beverage; it is quite amazing how the nerves of taste will respond with sheer delight to gratification of the unconscious needs of the body. It is said that they will react with the same keen pleasure to any sweet, any ordinary caramel, after a shot of insulin.

I now had private nurses, three of them, who relieved one another in day and night shifts of eight hours each. Their chief responsibility, aside from the injections of penicillin every three hours to prevent infection, was to help me in the very difficult task of turning myself about in bed, which the doctors had ordered: for movement, change of position, this way and that, without favouring the unwounded side, is part of present-day post-operative treatment. As early as the second day young Carlson made me stand without support beside my bed for a few minutes, although he stood by to catch me should I totter. It went very well, and my only trouble was returning via the stool to the rather high bed.

The night nurse who took the shift from eleven to seven was named June Colman. She was a remarkably endearing person. It is almost inevitable that the patient—even if he is old, sewed up, and difficult to turn—should develop a bit of warm feeling for the angel of his nights, if she is even only tolerably agreeable—and June was distinctly pretty.

In this too, I was "just another patient". At one or two o'clock in the morning, when I could no longer sleep and she brought me a cup of tea and the second seconal capsule ("the red capsule", was, of course, the only name for this excellent drug, which curiously enough cannot be procured in Europe), I might ask about her home, her training, her personal life. She was engaged, or had been engaged, for her fiancé had disappeared, had dropped out of sight, as she informed me with a shrug. Why in the world? Did she think he had taken up with another girl? "I wouldn't be surprised," she replied. "But I would be," I said. "I would be extremely surprised at such a blockhead!" I went that far, and she smiled gaily. She also had a very sweet, persuasive smile when I would huddle crossly and stubbornly in my armchair at night, no longer wanting to sleep or return to bed. After she had coaxed me into bed, propped the supporting pillow behind my back and with a safety pin fastened the button for the light signal to my blanket, she would take her leave for a half-hour at the night nurses' coffee break, saying: "Now I am going to have my coffee." The words "my coffee" were always said with such voluptuous tenderness that it gives me pleasure to this day to remember them.

Just as the operation had proceeded classically and uneventfully, in the clinical sense, so the convalescence progressed speedily and without complications. A man of thirty, the doctors assured me, could not have responded better. I was looked upon as a kind of prize patient. Of course I could still feel the shock that every operation of this sort imposes upon the nervous system and the whole organism. And a weakness in the chest had remained. Along with a strong tendency towards swallowing the wrong way it made clearing my throat and coughing up phlegm alarmingly difficult. Codeine was used to counter the unavoidable healing pains in the back. And the changes that had been undertaken in my interior, including removal of the seventh rib, upper displacement of the diaphragm, and similar rearrangements, created a certain shortness of breath when I moved too fast. But the oxygen apparatus which had stood for a while beside my bed soon vanished, and the frightfully long incision healed so well that good-looking young Carlson (good looks are a pleasure, whether in men or women) was able to remove the stitches after a few weeks—doing so with a skill that obviated the expected pain. He had moved from high school—the cultural aims of American high schools are not particularly ambitious—directly to medical school without attending college, and was receiving his education free, as a candidate for the Navy. Obviously, he knew nothing about anything except surgery, for which he had just as obviously been born and in which he was happy. I still see him in his rubber apron, pushing a stretcher on rubber wheels, with a sheet-swathed figure on it, at a youthful trot down the halls of Billings Hospital—a cheerfully one-sided, capable, and simple soul, good to look at.

Early in the morning, after June had bathed me skilfully as I lay and then, before she left, had brought me a cup of coffee (for breakfast did not come until nine o'clock), I would sit in my bathrobe at the window, watching the coming and going at the big main gate, noticing progress in the greening trees of the courtyard, reading and underlining Nietzsche's writings, for the lecture I still owed hovered over me as the next item on the agenda. Then Dr. Dallas B. Phemister, president of the American Surgeons Association and chief surgeon of the University Clinic, a representative of the best type in American scholarship, might drop in on me. He would inquire what I was doing, leaf through my Naumann edition of Nietzsche, and leave behind one or another article on medical history of which he was the author. Adams and his retinue then came on their regular round for the morning visit; my wife arrived, my daughters came, and in the course of the day or the days a good many visitors from outside found their way to me. Bermann and Gumpert called; Bruno Walter, who happened to be giving a concert in Chicago, sat by my bed; Caroline Newton likewise was not deterred by the distance between Chicago and New York, and brought gifts: a tea set for the afternoon, a fine woollen blanket. Alfred Knopf sent caviar. And there was never any lack of flowers. If they ever threatened to give out, Erika would come in bearing fresh roses. Surrounded in a critical situation by so much love, sympathy, solicitude, one asks oneself what one has done to deserve it—and pretty well asks in vain. Has any man who ever bore the incubus of creation upon his back, always concerned, obsessed, preoccupied with the work of days and years—has any such man ever been an enjoyable companion? *Dubito.* And I doubt it particularly for myself. How is it, then? Can the consciousness of one's arrears in this respect, the knowledge that one's work is claiming what one should be able to give freely to one's intimates—can the colouring of existence by this sense of guilt make up for the great lack and reconcile others to it, even win their affection? Here is a speculation impious enough to be ascribed to Adrian Leverkühn.

The novel—during all these alien, adventurous weeks I held it firmly in my heart, drew up in my mind a list of necessary improvements of what had already been written, and thought of its future course. My good conduct as a patient, the rapidity of my recovery, which seemed scarcely to befit my age—all this determination to withstand, and the simple fact of my having withstood, a belated and un-expected trial of my constitution—would not all this be secretly exposed to the question "What for?" if it were not for the service of the novel? And had I not summoned so much strength out of my depths in order to go and finish *that*? And yet, at the same time, the thought of the book was like an open wound; it needed only to be touched, even with the most loving intent, and in my weakness I would be shaken with unpredictable force. My wife and Erika had been reading the typewritten manuscript, which had come to Chicago with us, and while I sat in my bathrobe, without appetite, at my narrow little dining table, Erika spoke to me of her impression of certain incidents, the first visit of Spengler, Jeanette Scheurl, and Schwerdtfeger to Adrian in the village, of Rudi's artistic whistling, and how good she thought all of it was. Instantly I dissolved in tears—then had to explain to the child that they were tears of sheer joy, for she began forcefully reproaching herself for her lack of consideration.

Complete lack of appetite was the only symptom of which I still had to complain to the doctors, whose visits were growing more and more pointless. Partly this was due to the eternal doses of penicillin, which continued until the end of my stay at the hospital. That protective drug is surely praiseworthy, but in the long run, like the filth of the Harpies, it spoils food; after a while the whole world smells and tastes of penicillin, and the result is extreme disinclination for eating. In any case, a certain overfastidiousness of the senses is characteristic of this tender state of convalescence; sickness finds itself much too fine for many things that are quite acceptable to coarser conditions. Thus, I would have no traffic with spiritous beverages, a development that took me by surprise. The noblest imported wine, which Medi Borgese brought to my room, I either could not drink or could not taste. I was even too refined for the light American beer. What I drank in quantity at every meal was Coca-Cola—that popular beverage that is after all a great favourite with children, which I had never liked before and never had any taste for afterwards, but which suddenly became my one and only.

The return of my strength and my ability to move about freely was not delayed by these whims and refusals of the organism to co-operate with my mind. How hard it seemed, the first time, to conquer the short distance from the door of my room to the social room at the end of the corridor. Soon, on the arm of my wife or one of the afternoon nurses, I was covering many times this distance in my tour of all the corridors on the floor, where the names of doctors in demand somewhere constantly resounded from the loud-speakers. The day came when for the first time I again put on street clothes, was propelled in the wheel chair outside the building into the warming spring air, and even got out a little to take a moderate promenade in front of the hospital, then sit on a bench for a while, blanket over my knees. I read a great deal during my long hours in the horizontal. To start with it was the English edition of our Golo's excellent and much-praised book on Friedrich Gentz which occupied me. Later the Borgeses lent me the four volumes of *Green Henry*, which strangely, indeed scandalously, had remained virtually unknown to me until this moment. I knew Keller's correspondence with the publisher Vieweg, who had commissioned a novel and kept asking, insisting, refusing to understand such inability to complete the work, called it laziness, cheating, finally in all seriousness lost patience—while the young author, who had something unique growing under his hands, a book altogether out of the ordinary, of self-willed greatness that could only be developed over the course of years—the young author apologized, tried to explain, could not meet a single deadline, and was always applying for extensions. The comical conflict had amused me greatly, and yet I had never felt obliged to make more than a superficial, tentative acquaintanceship with a work belonging to so mighty a tradition and so akin to my own sphere. Was this connected with the fact that my youth had been shaped far more by European literature, Russian, French, Scandinavian, and English, rather than German, so that the encounter with Stifter had been delayed for such an amazingly long time? I believe that I knew no more than a few youthful episodes out of the whole of Keller's epic autobiography. Now I read with the greatest pleasure and sympathy, with ever growing admiration for the cleanly displayed wealth of vitality in the book, the delicious precision of its language, formed on the model of Goethe but altogether independent in its own right. I read with admiration, although there is in fact as little to admire about the narrator of the tale, Young Heinrich himself, that is, as about the heroes of other such novels of development —apparently there is a law governing this. Indeed, the epithet Goethe once gave to his Wilhelm Meister, "a poor dog", suits Heinrich even better than it does Wilhelm.

"You are still reading? Not sleeping? Shame on you!" It was June who said this when, coming in at eleven o'clock, she found my light still on. It was switched off; only the bluish glow of the night lamp remained; I assumed my sidewise sleeping position, bolstered by pillows, and the night angel sat down for her vigil in the chair which now so often served me, too, during the day. But I was weary of this existence, and well I might be weary of it. On one such night I conceived the exciting plan of not waiting it out here for the full six weeks after the operation; instead I would create a transitional stage and for the last few days before our departure would move into an hotel, the familiar Windermere, near the lake. Dr. Bloch was called and sounded out; he gave his consent.

The preparations were swiftly made, there followed a succession of hearty good-byes, autographing of books, gifts to the nurses; and a press conference, too, was quickly gone through. A number of reporters had gathered in our social and smoking room. Leaning on Erika's arm, still by no means in a fit state for talking at any length, I joined them—actually only eager to sing the praises of the institution, the doctors, and the glorious deeds they had performed upon me. But this was forbidden to me, since Billings Hospital tolerates no publicity and had even been extremely sparing of information concerning me during my stay. The result was that I could only recite for the benefit of the "boys" a few well-intentioned remarks on politics—and these were soon cut short by Erika, who was determined to save my strength. Medi Borgese drove us in her car to the hotel, where she had set up our headquarters. What splendid rooms! And the meals in our dinette—how much more appealing they were than the institutional food. I drank no more Coca-Cola. Dr. Bloch visited us in his off-hours. The railroad strike delayed our departure by twenty-four hours. There was a great deal of telephoning to determine whether and when the Chief would be leaving for Los Angeles. On Sunday it was ready. The return trip took place in the most comfortable circumstances; we had a drawing-room with private meals. On Tuesday, May 28, the three of us arrived back at Union Station.

XIV

It was the loveliest time of the year. The garden had been
beautifully looked after by Vattaru, and every stroll amidst
its rich display of flowers, every view over the valley and
hills to the clearly outlined chain of the Sierra and over the
tops of the palm trees on the other side to Catalina and the
ocean—all these paradisaical scenes and colours enraptured
me. I was happy to have kept my hold upon the natural
world, to have passed *cum laude* a rigorous test; happy to
have returned once again to the proper frame of my life, to
be united again with my books and with all the features of
an active, striving life; happy even at the joy of the poodle,
who must have sensed the grave meaning of our departure
and had laid his paw on my knee with so sad a look when I
sat in the bedroom awaiting the ambulance, and who now
celebrated our return with dances and wild dashes in circles;
happy above all over the decision, urged so strongly upon
me by Antonio Borgese, to concentrate for the present on
nothing but finishing the novel, which seemed to me in its
essentials already "closed in", as workmen say of a building. I had its course clearly in mind. Of course, it would
offer difficulties down to the last word, and some of them
big ones; but step by step it would be possible to overcome
them.

Good friends called and brought good gifts: the Dieterles, the Neumanns, Helene Thimig, Fritzi Massary.
Adorno sent Benjamin's book on German tragedy—among
its interesting points was one concerning the connection,
quite palpable here and there, between Shakespearean
drama and the allegorical devil gests of the Middle Ages.
According to Benjamin, the unequivocal comic aspects

(always brought out by great actors) in Shakespeare's arch-scoundrels and representatives of Evil incarnate, the Richards and Iagos, were magnificent relics of that sphere of religious humour, which did not lie so far away in time for their creator. I found this a brilliant and stimulating idea, with a great deal of bearing on my own book, where it deals with aspects of the satanic nature. It was in itself almost comic to observe this sharpness and alacrity about tracking down and picking out references, in whatever I happened to be reading, to my own passionate preoccupation. The truth is that, when one is at work, pertinent and significant material is constantly appearing from all sides, thrown across one's path as if fate were acting as procurer. Lion Feuchtwanger had little notion of what I was engaged on; yet his congratulatory gift was *Die Schriften des Agrippa von Nettesheim* (*The Writings of Agrippa of Nettesheim*)—a remarkably act of kindness, for I quickly found in it a quaintly denunciatory chapter on exorcism and black magic, and even more, one chapter on music, or rather against it, full of moralistic lore. According to the Greek poets, it seemed the God Jupiter had *never* sung, nor played the zither, and Pallas had cursed the flute. "To speak the honest truth, what is more useless, more contemptible, and more to be avoided than the pipers, the singers, and other suchlike music makers . . . who seek to enchant and capture the minds of men as it were by a poisoned sweet, like the sirens with their frivolous singing, *sham gestures*, and soft strains? Therefore did the wives of the brave Thracians persecute Orpheus, for with his songs he had made their husbands effeminate." Music has always been suspect, most suspect to those who loved it most deeply, like Nietzsche. . . .

A lot of talking produced shortness of breath and heavy

perspiration. The womenfolk insisted that I be spared exertion and above all have nothing to do with the accumulated mail; they themselves would go over it, along with the
secretary, loyal Hilde Kahn, the copyist of *Faustus*. Hospital
habits, like the nightly cup of tea taken along with sleep-
inducing drugs, and two hours of bed rest by day, persisted
for a time, partly because of sheer sentimentality. But only
two days after our return my resumed diary records: "Occupied with the last parts of the manuscript"; and at the
beginning of June I found myself happily working far back,
tinkering with and improving the for ever unsatisfactory
lecture chapter, VIII. Since sitting at the desk gave me
pains in the back, I was forced to take up a new working
posture, which I have maintained to the present day: writing in the corner of the sofa, the paper clipped to a board
resting on my lap. In this manner I spent the mornings,
making all the additions and changes that had come to me
while I was still in the hospital. Even before the middle of
the month I had gone through a list of these, and so the
moment for going forward had come. But there was still the
over-all criticism of "infernally long passages and liber-
ties", as the diary expresses it, with the careless coda: "Let
others cut them out." This disposition to let others take
responsibility for further operations, which presumably
would have to be of a strenuous sort, was probably due to
my convalescent state. I was being easy on myself. But this
was also connected with my secret conception of the work
as a legacy. I felt as though I personally need take no
thought of its publication and could allow editor and executor to proceed as they wished. For a time at least, this
was my view. Incidentally, in taking that view I no doubt
already had in mind the one person about me to whom the
paternal words of Wotan might apply: "When I speak with

you, I consult only with myself"—she who would know precisely what I had meant.

For the present, it was good to be moving ahead. The middle of June had not yet arrived when I began writing Chapter XXXV, the fate of poor Clarissa—freely following life, the actuality of my own sister's suicide. Twelve days later it was completed, so that before the end of the month I was able to begin the next chapter, recalling the atmosphere of the twenties in Germany and introducing the invisible friend, that model of deepest discretion. I amused myself describing her gift of the ring. My seventy-first birthday had meanwhile come. The practical and most useful gift it brought me was a handsome folding chair, which now accompanied us on outings, to serve as a place of rest for me in the open air at favourite sites with a view of the ocean. I still had some difficulty walking, and my innate incapacity for thinking beyond the present condition led me to imagine that from now to the end of my days I should have to go out with that folding chair—when, in fact, it quickly became a thing of the past.

In *L'Arche*, the magazine founded by Gide, which came to me regularly, I read an instructive study of Anton von Webern, Schönberg's disciple. The article spoke well for the French intellectual's appreciation of modern music. In addition, there was a perceptive essay on Nietzsche's atheism, regarded as a special form of religion. This fitted in with the conception which I had found much to my liking ever since I encountered it in American critical writing: that Nietzsche's struggle against Christian morality constituted an event *within* the history of Christianity.

Stephen Spender had travelled through shattered Germany; his lively report on it appeared in German in the *Neue Schweizer Rundschau* and caused some stir by its descriptions of German writers, who in their tragic effusions over their fate only revealed their moral flabbiness, their emotional conceit—a new and disturbing exposé of the conduct of the Inner Emigration. The article might have been called, *Under Western Eyes*, like Joseph Conrad's masterpiece—I was nowadays reading a great deal, perhaps all, of him before going to sleep. I had begun with *Lord Jim*, continued with *Victory*, and in the course of several weeks read through the whole series of these novels, entertained, impressed, and as a German somehow shamed by his manly, adventure-loving, linguistically superior, and psychologically and morally profound narrative art. To say that this art is rare with us is false—we simply do not have it.

I was still reading *Green Henry*, which, it occurred to me, was also related through Goethe with Adalbert Stifter's *Nachsommer*. Admirable to the very end. In my ignorance of literary history, I was puzzled and intrigued by the discrepancies within the fourth volume in the edition I had read in the hospital. It was obvious that here were two versions, and the disparity extended back into the third part, for even the "combat of fools" has different conclusions, since in one version Lys sustains a wound from which he afterwards dies. And how strange, occurring nowhere else, was the later abandonment of the autobiographical form, the transition from the first to the third person! Fortunately, one June day a Zürich friend called on us, the young writer Richard Schweizer, who had film business on this coast. I launched a complaint about these discords, made him answerable for them; and a few weeks later, when he had bounded back to Zürich, what should arrive from him but eight handsomely printed, clothbound volumes consisting of the two versions of the splendid work that Jonas Fränkel had published "on the basis of the posthumous papers": the editions of 1926 and of 1854, which now stand on a shelf in my study and which clarify the perplexing problem.

A gratifying report came from Germany. They had held a series of lectures on *Lotte in Weimar*, where but in Weimar, and moreover in the social rooms of the Goethe house —this under Russian sponsorship. If I was correctly informed, the lectures had been thronged. The incident touched me deeply. Incidentally, it had a comical counterpart which I heard about somewhat later. Even during the war, copies of the novel had been smuggled in from Switzerland and circulated widely. In the long monologue of the seventh chapter there occur authentic and documented sayings of Goethe side by side with apocryphal matter of my own invention, to which, of course, I gave a Goethean cast. Opponents of the régime had extracted from this monologue a number of dicta which analysed the German character in unfavourable terms and warned that it might lead to evil; these passages had been collected and distributed as a leaflet under the camouflage title of *From Goethe's Conversations with Riemer*. A copy or a translation of the curious forgery fell into the hands of the British prosecutor at the Nuremberg trials, Sir Hartley Shawcross. In good faith, impressed by the topical forcefulness of the remarks, he quoted extensively from it in his charge. He was not to escape unscathed. Soon the London *Times Literary Supplement* carried an article demonstrating that Shawcross had not been quoting from Goethe but from my novel—which produced some embarrassment in London official circles. At the request of the Foreign Office the British ambassador in Washington, Lord Inverchapel, wrote to me asking for an explanation. In my reply I admitted that *The Times* had been right; the whole affair was due to a well-meant mystification on the part of the pamphleteers. But I could warrant, I declared, that if Goethe had not really said the words the prosecutor attributed to him, he might very well have said them. In a higher sense, therefore, Sir Hartley had quoted correctly.

This little comedy of errors took place somewhat later, in midsummer. It was still June when a far more serious and more moving item of news came from Germany. We learned that on the sixth of that month, my birthday, that is, Gerhart Hauptmann had died. It was quite some time before I heard the details: how Hauptmann, eighty-four years old, had been compelled to leave his home in the Silesian mountains, which had been requisitioned by the Poles; and how, in the midst of the household's dissolution, with all the bags packed, he had lain down and died. My thoughts turned frequently to this departed colleague, to our many meetings, which occasionally, in Bolzano and at Hiddensee, involved our living together under the same roof. I thought of that unique, partly farcical but always moving, engaging personality, towards whom one always felt affection and reverence. Undoubtedly there had been something sham, something decidedly empty, about that personality. Because of its intellectual limits, there was a quality of unfinished development about it; it had a greatness that was never completed, never fully articulated, that remained masklike. You could hang for hours on the lips of the man, strangely spellbound, as he talked on with many gestures, his snow-white hair flying, and yet from all the talk scarcely anything would "come out". In some circumstances, however, something would come out; it might be very simple, but the personality brought it into sharp relief, elevated it to a new and powerful truth that you never forgot.

One evening in Hiddensee, perhaps in the summer of 1923, he had read to us from his *Till Eulenspiegel* epic. He selected that uncanny song in which the sun neglects to rise. After we had discussed this a while, he asked me to read something from *The Magic Mountain*—I was then about three-quarters into it. I refused. I felt honestly disinclined to read after he had read, and said so. At that he became quite agitated. There was something of a performance before he brought out the idea that was working inside him. First came an elaborate pantomime of protests, gestures of dismay, compelling signals for attention. Then it came: "Dear friend. . . . Not so. . . . You are wrong. . . . In our Father's house are many mansions!" That was so good, so neatly found and cleanly felt a phrase, so magnificently thought and proper to the occasion, that it touched me to the heart. He responded to my applause with a repeated. contented, "It's so, isn't it? It's so, isn't it?" And so I no longer resisted. I read something I had written recently, the chapter "By the Ocean of Time", a thoroughly abstract piece of semi-humorous philosophy that does not do very well taken out of context. His secretary, Fräulein Jungmann, who was present, was dreadfully bored. But it appealed to the old man. In listening he had paid close attention to the intonation, the language, the intellectual rhythm, and he made stylistic comparisons. "What it most reminds me of," he said, "is Meredith." I have remembered that remark because it tells a great deal of his sensitivity to rhythmic resemblances and affinities. Indeed, he himself was a great rhythmic artist; long ago Richard Dehmel pointed out the hidden metrics, the inner verse, of his supposedly naturalistic Silesian popular speech. The weight of his writing often, as at the end of *Michael Kramer*, falls almost entirely upon the language, almost without thoughts, or with thought of extremest vagueness. Once he remarked that the beginning of Hofmannthal's *Andreas* fragment had been influenced by the style of Georg Büchner's *Lenz*. A purely rhythmic insight that scarcely anyone else would have hit on.

I must also tell a little anecdote about his good nature and solicitude. At Hiddensee he used to take his swim at a very early hour. One morning, when I came down to the beach, I found him already there, his white hair pasted to his head, clothed in a bathrobe, and drying himself. We exchanged greetings, and I asked casually: "How was the water?" "Very pleasant," he replied. "Only a little warm." "So much the better!" I said, and walked on. I had gone about fifteen paces when he literally come trotting after me, repeatedly and insistently calling my name. When I turned around, he explained, a little breathlessly: "I must tell you I was joking. The water is frightfully cold." Obviously, he had feared I might suffer an uncomfortable shock.

A good man. And a happy man during the greater part of his life. When he was in Munich for the celebration of his seventieth birthday (a celebration that went on for weeks), we had a champagne breakfast with him in the Hotel Continental. With us was Max Halbe, who always addressed him as "my great friend", with much-trilled r's. The breakfast stretched on into one of Hauptmann's beloved drinking sessions; it lasted from half past one until six o'clock. He was as magnificent and as significantly insignificant in his talk as ever. Whenever there loomed the danger of some serious discussion, he would break it off with a resolute: "Boys, instead let's drink some more of this innocuous stuff!" The innocuous stuff was Moët-Chandon. With a heavy cargo, he was finally taken in the lift to his room, where he lay down and fell asleep instantly—actually before the person who had seen him to bed could close the door. The festival performance of *The Rats* was to begin at the theatre at eight o'clock. He came to his box a good twenty minutes late, was acclaimed like a king by the patiently waiting audience, sat down, and watched the entire performance—a splendid performance of what is perhaps his best play—with the greatest pleasure.

A happy man, a man of blessings. And he wanted to remain so. He declined the role of martyr. He called unconditional struggle against the rising racial barbarism "graceless"—a carefully chosen word with connotations both of ungracious and unblessed. Probably, too, he thought he ought to follow the example of Goethe, who had said:

> It pleases me to hold converse
> With clever men, with tyrants.

Clever men! And with bloodstained blockheads, too? Hauptmann was ready even for that. As far as he was concerned, the seizure of power did not have to change anything. He did not want to lose his representative role. He wanted to celebrate his eightieth birthday as he had his seventieth. He remained in Germany, raised the swastika flag, wrote *I say Yes!* and even went so far as to have an audience with Hitler, who for one shameful minute bored his stupid basilisk's gaze into those small, pale, thoroughly un-Goethean eyes, before "stalking" on. Around 1900 Maximilian Harden used to call the Germanic pet of Jewish critics "poor Herr Hauptmann". Now he was really poor Herr Hauptmann. Isolated, embittered, and on top of all despised by the Nazis themselves for his willingness to capitulate, he must have suffered unspeakably in the stifling air, the bloody vapours, of the Third Reich, must have sorrowed unspeakably over the ruin of the country and the people he loved. His last photographs show the features of a martyr; he became what had wished not to be. Those pictures floated painfully before my mind at the news of his passing, and I felt his death the harder because of the perception that for all the difference in our natures, and for all that life and events had led us far apart, we had been friends after a fashion. I do not deny the element of irony that was mixed with my admiration for him. But just as this admiration came from the heart, so he in his turn probably esteemed the mansion that I occupied "in our Father's house". He knew of the jest on personality that I had permitted myself in *The Magic Mountain*, the symbol of majestic inadequacy that I had constructed after his image; but in spite of all the chatterboxes, in spite of various endeavours to force him to take notice of the portrait, to stir him up against me, he always overlooked the thing with magnificent tolerance. In 1925 he publicly praised the book in high terms; and the fact that the Nobel Prize came my way in 1929 was due considerably, and perhaps primarily, to his work. He telephoned me in Munich from Schreiberhau to tell me that he had just had a decisive telephone conversation with the kingmaker in Stockholm, Professor Böök of the Swedish Academy, and that he was happy to be the first to congratulate me. I replied that I would cherish the distinction all the more, the more I owed it to him. . . .

Friends, but yet we always stood on a formal footing with each other. The oddest, most comic moment in our association was the time he was on the point of proposing that we address each other with the familiar *Du*. He had probably been drinking a good deal, and began: "Well, then. . . . Consider that. . . . Good! . . . We are brothers after all, aren't we? . . . Shouldn't we therefore. . . . Certainly. . . . But let it pass!" The polite *Sie* remained. And yet—who else could he with more reason have called his brother?

Slowly my nervous system recuperated. But what I had for more than a year not succeeded in doing now took place effortlessly: every week, without relapse or pause, the scales showed a gain in weight of one and a half or two pounds. Such a biological upswing often follows operations. Possibly it was aided in this case by a new wonder drug, a recent Russian discovery, which Dr. Rosenthal gave me by injection several times—incidentally, it affected my arm badly, left an itching red patch. The diary makes note of "crucial psychological and technical preparations for war in this country". But side by side with that, quite unconcerned, it continues to mention steady progress on the novel, which by the middle of July had proceeded as far as the Fitelberg chapter, or my accumulating material for it. I had long had in mind the character of the international impresario, had long ago conceived of the symbolic temptation from solitude exerted by the "world". As for the idea of doing the scene as a long monologue by the amusing tempter, with the reactions of his hearers merely hinted at —that came to me at once, as soon as I had assembled the materials for the conversation.

What I still lacked, what I could not yet picture, was the person himself, the man's appearance. But here, too, help came at the proper moment. One morning, over early coffee in my bedroom, I talked to my wife about this minor yet troublesome concern, which reminded me of those distant days in Bolzano when I was in a quandary about how to make something picturesque out of Mynheer Peeperkorn. Once again my wife had good advice. The very type was more or less at hand, she said; I need only recall the general lineaments of an old friend of mine in New York, formerly active in Paris as a literary and theatrical agent (though, it is true, he had nothing to do with music). He could supply the face for my man of the world. Excellent! Of course, he was the one. How could I have failed to think of him! It is always the greatest of pleasures to work from nature, spiritualizing, exaggerating, and intensifying; and any protest of unlikeness I could counter with Liebermann's reply: "That is a better likeness than you yourself."

From then on the standing note is: "Working on XXXVII." "Working on Fitelberg all day." And although in between I gave several days to an article which had been commissioned by *Musical Quarterly* for Bruno Walter's seventieth birthday, and which I wrote in the form of a friendly letter, I was able to finish the chapter by the middle of August, little more than three weeks after beginning it. It provides a refreshing episode amid all the gloom and makes very effective reading aloud, since the character has something of the gay equivocation and theatrical dash of a Riccaut de la Marlinière. Lessing's handling of this character, it is true, laid him open to the charge of malicious, jingoistic calumny of France. And since I had always thought that here he had indeed been guilty of a certain moral frivolity for the sake of an effect, I also had to be cognizant of the danger of an anti-Semitic misinterpretation of my Jewish Riccaut, despite the sympathetic drollness with which I endowed my character. It was at the first reading of the section before members of the family and close friends that my attention was called to this danger. And, surprising as the idea was to me, I had to grant its validity—all the more so since the book's cast of characters also includes the nasty figure of Breisacher, an intellectual intriguer and forerunner of evil, the characterization of whom gives grounds for the same suspicion. Of him, incidentally, I had written: "Yet can one quarrel with the Jewish spirit when its quick hearing and receptivity for the coming thing, the new, persists also in the most extraordinary situation, where the avant-garde coincides with the reactionary?" And of Fitelberg: "I have the Old Testament in my bones, a thing no less serious-minded than being German. . . ." The first segment makes the point that my Jews are simply children of their age, just as much as the others; that, indeed, by virtue of their cleverness they are often the more faithful children. And the second brings out the peculiar spiritual dignity of Judaism, which may seem to be insufficiently appreciated in the book but to which I paid my respects when I drew the picture of the cosmopolitan Jewish impresario. For that matter, leaving out Mother Schweigestill and the narrator himself, Serenus Zeitblom, are the German inhabitants of this novel any more likeable than the Jewish characters? It is, on the whole, a strange aquarium of creatures of the Last Days! I certainly prefer Fitelberg to the pure German phantoms at Kridwiss's who discuss the times and their humours. As long, therefore, as one cannot call the novel anti-German (though there were those who did so), so also it cannot be called in any sense anti-Semitic.

Now, after the middle of August, while I was beginning on Chapter XXXVIII, dealing with the violin sonata and the conversation at Bullinger's, there began the editorial sessions with Erika. She had been doing a good deal of work on the typescript, which had been recalled from Mrs. Lowe, and was lovingly bent on freeing it from draggingly long sections, needless difficulties for the translator, and burdensome pedantries that by myself I would not have had the resolution to eliminate. Now we turned to the manuscript, especially the early portions, and hewed away at the product of so many mornings' labour—with reluctance always on the side of the editor, who found everything so beautifully written, a pity to lose this or that, and whose only thought was that the whole might gain by such sacrifices. No doubt she had expected that I would fight for every line and was surprised at my docility—an old trait in me that had only to be reawakened. There was scarcely any bargaining or haggling. "Why, yes. Certainly. Out with it! We'll cut a page and a half; we'll cut three pages. That will make it more readable, *somewhat* more readable." Some further operations were performed on the chapter of Kretschmar's lectures. Music theory was flung overboard. The student conversations were pruned. The over-indulgence in Brentano songs was cut back. In the chapter on theology at Halle, an entire professor and his course were liquidated.

Finally, after many a going-over on the part of this shrewd counsellor, the manuscript had been lightened by some forty pages—and precisely the right ones. No one misses them; I do not miss them, either. Taking them out, eliminating them, was a weight off my heart. The only drawback was that I was held up awhile by the necessity to hide the breaks and build little bridges where connections had been broken. This done, a large batch of finally finished manuscript could be sent off once more to the translator in Oxford, England.

Concerning the violin concerto, Adrian's ambiguous gift to overfamiliarity, I had already given a description of the work fairly in keeping with its peculiar psychological significance, when Adorno inquired about it. "The concerto you spoke about—have you come to it yet?" "I am pretty well into it." "Well, if you will allow me—this is important; this is something we want to be quite accurate about." And in a few words he briefed me on the technical aspects of the opus, the "parody of being carried away", of which I had had only a very impressionistic idea.

Chapter XXXVIII was done in twelve days, and two days after completing it I began the next; opening in Zürich, it introduced Marie Godeau into our story, which from now on grows more and more novelistic, that is to say, dramatic. We spent the evening of that day celebrating Bruno Walter's birthday at the home of Alma Mahler-Werfel, along with the Arlts, Fritzi Massary, and Oskar Karlweis. Our gift to him, who was on the point of leaving for his first European tour since the war, was an edition of Grillparzer for the library of his new house in Beverly Hills. Our old friend was touched when, after dinner, I read to the group in German my article for the *Musical Quarterly* and presented him with the manuscript. After all, I was giving him no more than I had received from him, for at bottom my little essay only paraphrased his memoirs, *Theme and Variations*, which had just been published in English and in which he so genially recalls our first acquaintanceship and neighbourly relations in Munich's Herzog Park.

The evening was one of great merriment because of Karlweis, who gave liberally of his pre-eminent comic talent. He has a priceless private number, a take-off on the Viennese actor Moser. It is a bravura bit of comic monologue, about ten minutes long and chiefly concerned with the fact that "all the schillings are in New York, and that is the difficulty". Anyone who has heard it will know that we wept tears of laughter. I cannot say how grateful I am for the gifts of a genuine *vis comica*. A social group that includes one of the virtuosi of such comedy is safe. I at any rate give thanks when one is present, for I have unlimited admiration for well-aimed parody, and I never tire of such demonstrations. That is why I greet Charlie Chaplin with such joy at a party. His creative mimicry, enormously graceful and sure in aim as it is, quickly makes him the centre of attention, and the evening is certain to be brilliant. We were meeting him quite often during this period, at Salka Viertel's, say, or at Florence Homolka's. And I cannot forget, for example, the description he once gave of his youthful success. He told of a trip he had made from Hollywood to New York, still unaware of his enormous fame, and of the fantastic situations into which his wild and boundless popularity cast him. The story as he told it was a masterpiece of grotesque narration. But this same genius of a clown—I do not want to omit this—listened with the keenest attention when in response to his questions I told him something about my work, about the novel now approaching its end, for he had heard about it. "That's fascinating!" he said. "This may well be your greatest book."

Some time after August 20, while I was busily making notes in preparation for the Adrian-Marie-Rudi-Inez drama, a real plot that even includes the excitement of a murder of jealousy, we had various visitors. Medi Borgese came for a stay with us, accompanied by her two English-speaking little daughters, and my joy in these charming grandchildren was no less intense, though somewhat less patent, than my pleasure in the Swiss boys. The elder girl is a charming little Mediterranean princess with a delightful intelligence; Dominica, the smaller one, even more like her father, with the face of a Sicilian peasant child, droll, possesses a curious sense of dignity such as is rarely found in children. She can scarcely bear it when grown-ups laugh at her, and will turn to her mother with a deep-felt and

almost stern question: "Why do they laugh?" Her tone
suggests that she wishes to say: "Have I made myself rid-
iculous in any way?" To which you can only respond with a
host of assurances that the laughter had nothing to do with
her and that her little person is taken altogether seriously.

Curiously enough, this was the time for a reunion with
the hospital era, or rather with one of its striking personalities. Professor Bloch of Chicago and his wife came as our
guests. He checked over the scar and the healing processes,
and found me in the most satisfactory condition. Indeed,
the gain in weight was continuing steadily, although soon
after Bloch's visit I was troubled by a malady which I had
had once before, years ago in Zürich, after a case of erysip-
elas, that is, again after a long confinement in bed. This
bout of it, however, was far more violent than the earlier
one. It was an extremely tormenting, itching, and inflamed
skin disease which wrought havoc with my sleep. It started
around the beginning of September, often producing un-
bearable irritation, and dragged on deep into October. It
is well known that these semi-nervous (but also extremely
real) afflictions are difficult to treat. Under certain circumstances X-ray radiation or anaesthetic drugs do more harm
than good. Nevertheless, I applied for help to doctor after
doctor, both American and German. All of them failed;
with the best will in the world, they only made matters
worse. During these weeks of suffering I had a strange experience that reminded me somewhat of Adrian's star-
crossed visits to the doctors in Leipzig. One day I arrived
at the Medical Building in Beverly Hills, where the man I
had just set my hopes upon had his offices, to find that the
place had been burned out over night and could no longer
be entered. Nothing was left but blackened, water-stained
walls, filth, and general desolation. Perhaps it was my good

fortune that providence obstructed one more of these well-intentioned and probably very skilful but unfortunately baneful treatments. Finally I landed in the hands of a mouse-eyed little Russian Jewish woman in the remote reaches of Los Angeles. It was quite a trip to reach her office, and she was so overworked and her schedule had fallen into such hopeless disorder that one had to wait for hours. But she knew her speciality thoroughly—this was it, and she relieved me at once and in the course of a few weeks cured me.

"Even without sleep I will work," my diary reads defiantly on one occasion. And it is true that even during the worst of it, the maddening malady was unable to affect the progress of the novel. My task was too close to completion, I was too filled with it, and too sure now of what I was doing. I took off a day or two towards the end of September in order to write a foreword for a novel by Bohuš Beneš, nephew of our friend and patron, the Czech President; the book, *God's Village*, was being published in England, and my foreword was in the form of a letter. Then I went on, morning after morning, spinning my thread, reeling out the mythic drama of the woman and the two friends in its weird special variation. I told of Adrian's announcement of his desire to marry, of the wintry outing into the Bavarian mountains; I did the dialogue between Adrian and Schwerdtfeger in Pfeiffering (Chapter XLI), an enigmatic affair with diabolic elements lurking in the background. During the composition of these passages the diary repeatedly notes: "Reading Shakespeare." I added the scenes between Rudi and Marie preceding the engagement, and after the middle of October finished with ease (how easy it is to deal with catastrophic happenings!) Chapter XLII, the shooting in the tram. A few days later, while reading these sections aloud at the Neumanns' in Hollywood, I became aware of how long my imagination had been harbouring the idea of such an incident, where the electric fires that flash and hiss under the wheels and at the top of the contact pole of a tram-car presage the murder that is to be committed. The concept belonged to the group of ancient, never executed ideas for novels which I referred to at the beginning of this account. For some fifty years I had been carrying around inside of me the vision of these cold flames before I finally found a place for it in a late work that had incorporated a good many elements out of the emotional world of those early days.

Incidentally, Kitty Neumann saved me from making a serious boner as regards the Munich scene. I had had the murder take place on a car of Line 1—which, it seemed, never went out to Schwabing. There were several other tram lines which would answer the need, and so the text now reads "Line 10," thanks to the alertness of this listener, who at once pointed out the mistake in accents sprung from the very soil of Munich.

Once again the folks from San Francisco came down, and the notation appears: "Drew for Frido a palm, a railroad, a cello player, a burning house." The diary now contains several descriptions of the winsome child, already represented in a transfigured, disembodied manner, and with the adjective "elfin". "Seems like an elf." "Spent the morning with the elfin little fellow on my balcony . . ." His hour was approaching. Chapter XLII, and with it the next to the last part of the book, was concluded towards the end of October. On the last day of the month, Chapter XLIII, the chamber-music chapter, was begun, already leading into the Lamentation oratorio, the creation of which was to be delayed by the appearance and the agonizing departure of the marvellous child. Yet how many preoccupying events, both political and personal, how many reading experiences, social encounters, and matters unfolding via the mail, for ever interfered with my main activity, the current work. For, after all, only three or four hours of the day belonged to it, although these were the best hours and hermetically sealed off from anything else.

As far as reading was concerned, the novels of Conrad still seemed the most appropriate to the present stage of my own novel—or, at any rate, the entertainment that least disturbed it. I read *The Nigger of the Narcissus*, *Nostromo*, *The Arrow of Gold*, *An Outcast of the Islands*, and the rest of those excellent books, read them with great pleasure. But I also turned to things of a wholly different sort, like E.T.A. Hoffmann's *The Elemental Spirit*, and purely philological matter which fed and stimulated my linguistic imagination, like *Sprichwörter des Mittelalters* (*Proverbs of the Middle Ages*) by the venerable Samuel Singer of Bern.

In September the conflict between Henry Wallace and Secretary Byrnes had broken out, and the Secretary of Commerce, whose speech on foreign policy had endangered the "peace work" of Paris, was dropped by Roosevelt's successor and creature. "Praised by Reds" was the stigma attached to Wallace, and before very long the man from Iowa was being challenged, more or less rhetorically, to register as a foreign agent. The night the radio announced his resignation we sent him a telegram of sympathy.

Churchill's Pan-Europe speech in Zürich, urging Franco-German co-operation under American and Russian sponsorship, also came at this time. It was exceeded, in suspect pro-Germanism, by the remarks in Stuttgart of the American Secretary of State. More clearly than ever before one could see emerging the desire to rearm Germany against Russia, together with the personal hopes of the old warrior for "one more gallant fight".

Towards the beginning of November the Congressional elections took place, the Republicans gaining a victory with some fifty-five per cent of the votes. The European view was that Truman had brought his party into disrepute and that, in contrast to the rest of the world, America stood far to the right. It could not remain where it had been standing. Powerful interests were at work thoroughly demolishing the work of Roosevelt. They were stirring up anger and regret that America had joined with Russia to defeat Germany, instead of joining with Germany against Russia. How far would this regressive movement carry? To the point of fascism? To war? This, too, was something to consider, the daily developments to be carefully followed and evaluated. It all belonged, like the events of recent years, to the background of this novel of a novel.

A more personal event of the latter part of September had its political overtones. The mail brought a letter from a former professor at Bonn, now working in London, who was commissioned to sound me out as to whether I would once more accept the honorary doctorate of the Bonn Philosophical Faculty, which had been rescinded in the Nazi era. My reply was a natural and conciliatory, "Why, gladly!" Yet I cherished the thought that what I had had to say back in 1936 to my fellow countrymen and the world on the occasion of my national and academic excommunication —in the "Bonn Letter", that is—would, God be praised, because of this act of restitution not vanish from memory.

Within a short time, then, I received the solemn Latinate diploma of 1919, my first copy of which had long since gone astray—it came in two copies, no less, accompanied by extremely cordial letters from the rector and the dean of the university.

A young Chicago student, member of an association for the propagation of the World Government idea, deeply disturbed by the outcome of the elections, by the path his country had chosen, came to see me one September afternoon. In the course of our long talk we discussed the threat of the atom bomb and the necessity of international control in much the same terms as were employed, several weeks later, in the proclamations on this fateful question by Einstein and seven other physicists. The young man urged me to come to Chicago and speak to his organization on the necessity for establishing a world authority for the safeguarding of peace. Such a journey was out of the question for me, but I promised him a statement, or, as we say more solemnly in German, a message on peace as the supreme commandment. In the new situation, I would say, utopia had become a question of practical life. I actually did interrupt work on the current chapter in order to keep my promise to this representative of sensitive youth—though I was certain that my declaration would be swallowed up by the tides of nemesis even more quickly, would vanish with even less of a trace than the great scientist's manifesto.

Musical Quarterly, in acknowledgment of my recent contribution, presented me with a curious book containing facsimile reproductions of letters of Beethoven in American collections. I looked at them for a long time, those scrambled and scratched lines hurled onto the paper, that desperate orthography, all that half-wild inarticulateness—and could find no love for it in my heart. Once again I sympathized with Goethe's rejection of the "untamed human soul", and once again gave thought to the relationship between music and intellect, music and good breeding, music and

171

humanity. Has musical genius, then, nothing at all to do with humanity and "better society"? Does it perhaps work directly in opposition to these? But Beethoven was a man with faith in revolutionary humanitarianism, and French writers have taken him to task for employing, as a musician, the language of a radical politician. . . . Say what you will, the French are aesthetes. I became aware of that once more by comparing two books, one German and one French, whose subject was my own work and which reached me almost simultaneously that autumn. The title of the French one (by Jean Fougère) links my name with the idea of *Séduction de la Mort.* The German book on the other hand, a study by Arnold Bauer, published in the East Zone, speaks of my work in connection with the "crisis of bourgeois culture"! Does the French intellectual have any serious notion of that crisis? Just after the First World War, so it seems to me, he has left it to the Germans "to dream apocalypses" and has instead become intrigued by such aesthetic matters as "seduction by death". It is not entirely accurate to say that the German mind is metaphysical and the French social.

We had Schönberg to our house one evening, and this is the place to mention it. He told me about the new trio he had just completed, and about the experiences he had secretly woven into the composition—experiences of which the work was a kind of fruit. He had, he said, represented his illness and medical treatment in the music, including even the male nurses and all the other oddities of American hospitals. The work was extremely difficult to play, he said, in fact almost impossible, or at best only for three players of virtuoso rank; but, on the other hand, the music was very rewarding because of its extraordinary tonal effects. I worked the association of "impossible but rewarding" into the chapter on Leverkühn's chamber music.

A letter to Dr. Rosenthal asking for information on the course of meningitis was dispatched at the end of October. Early in November I began work on the first Echo chapter (XLIV). Day after day I wrote away at it. I described the frail little boy in all his elfin charm. I took the tenderness of my own heart and transformed it into something no longer entirely rational, endowing the child with a loveliness which was somehow divine, so that people felt him as a visitor from some high and faraway realm, an epiphany. I had the little messenger make his strange pronunciamentos, patterning these on the voice and the accents of the angelic little chap which rang clearly in my own ear. At least one of those curious phrases, the "Well, you are glad I did come, yes?" was actually spoken at one time. The whole act of transformation and transcendence that I was undertaking is comprised in the beautiful, transparent double meaning which this "come" assumes, as if of its own accord. At the same time I felt under a curiously dreamlike spell at the way the book, which after all is essentially a book concerning Germanism, took on, by way of the child's speech, a new linguistic reach, penetrating beyond the baroque and the German of Luther, deep into Middle High German. For Echo's evening prayers, whose source none of the characters in the novel can identify, I used sayings from Freidank's *Bescheidenheit* (*Wisdom*) (thirteenth century), which I adapted as prayers usually by rephrasing the third and fourth verses. The little modern verses Echo recites I drew from memory of an old picture book that I myself had been attached to as a child.

I do not believe I have ever worked with more eagerness. "On the Echo chapter", is the diary jotting for many days in succession. "Hard at work from very early in the morning." "Much reading of *The Tempest*." "Slept restlessly from too much intellectual work at night." Then, early in December: "Working on Echo's fatal disease, sorrowing." "Sorrowing!" The phrase was repeated often now; it became a regular thing. The "divine child" was to be snatched away from the man who was not permitted love, the man of "coldness"; that had long ago been decided and was the inescapable necessity. I had prepared myself for it by obtaining precise information on the disease by which the Evil One accomplished his end. But to carry out the task was bitterly hard for me. When, later in London, the translator asked me in all seriousness, "How could you do it?" I answered her that she could read my own feelings in Adrian's behaviour, in his use of the phrase "it is not to be", in his break with hope, and his saying, "It will be taken back".

One day before the middle of December came the diary note: "Chapter XLV finished as it must be, no help for it." The next day contained the note: "Rose early, deeply troubled by the state of the book, by the prospective reading of what I have last written, and by what yet remains to be done." My wife's twin brother, Klaus Pringsheim, with his son, had come from Tokyo on a visit to the States. For years he had been conductor of the imperial orchestra there. He had been staying with us for several weeks. One evening, in his presence and that of our Golo, who had just become a professor of history at Pomona College, I read this sweet and fearful episode. It is probably the most poetic moment the novel attains, and I read it with an emotion which the listeners obviously felt. We spoke a good deal about the ethereal and heartbreaking incident, and told one another that the chapter must be kept as long as possible from the mother of the actual child—who incidentally was a strapping youngster well beyond Echo's age.

The artist always carries a work of art as a whole within himself. Although aesthetics may insist that literary and musical works, in contradistinction to the plastic arts, are dependent upon time and succession of events, it is nevertheless true that even such works strive at every moment to be present as a whole. Middle and end are alive in the beginning, the past suffuses the present, and even the greatest concentration upon the moment does not obviate concern for the future. Thus, while the story of the child seemed to absorb me completely, I was already looking towards what was to follow immediately, the depiction of Leverkühn's second major work, *The Lamentation of Dr. Faustus*. An entry at the time I was still busy with the first Echo chapter reads: "Drawing on the chapbook for ideas for the Faust oratorio. The whole thing to be choric, historically linked to the *lamento* of the seventeenth century, breakthrough from formal construction to expression." Around the same time: "Talking with Adorno about the cantata. . . Adornos for dinner. Later in the studio, I read the conversation in Pfeiffering and Rudolf's death. Again and again, I see how this work is a parallel to *Parsifal*, in its relationship to all that precedes." And then comes one of those cries from the depths such as occur from time to time in the entries of those years: "The fact remains, never before has any work so agitated and moved me!"

Now on the agenda was the dramatization of the process of "retrieving", and I well recall the productive November afternoon that I spent discussing this urgent matter with my musical friend and adjutant. Our conversation at first revolved around the fourth volume of Ernest Newman's great biography of Wagner, which I had asked Knopf for, probably just for its account of *Parsifal*. I was thoroughly dissatisfied with Newman's psychological explanation of

Nietzsche's break with Wagner (which he attributes to ordinary jealousy, and even simply social envy). Newman has little respect for Wagner as a thinker, no more than he has for Nietzsche, but he forgives Wagner everything for the sake of his works—as though these had nothing to do with thinking. Moreover, he once calls his hero "a born amateur"—yet does not realize that this aspect of Wagner, and with it the tendency towards authoritarian pronouncements on everything and anything, the inordinate immodesty which anticipated Hitler's, was precisely what got on Nietzsche's nerves. The epithet, incidentally, could only please me. What an outcry there was when in my *Suffering and Greatness of Richard Wagner* I had called the man who advocated the "total work of art" a dilettante of genius. Now here was the same bold phrase used in a four-volume biography by an undoubted expert on the subject.

Enough of that. We passed on to the cantata. For this, the "Privy Councillor", as I was to call Adorno in the dedication I penned upon his copy of the book, had thought up many valuable ideas. And yet I am tempted to say that his chief contribution to the chapter lay not in the musical sphere but in the realm of language and its nuances, especially, where, at the end, the chapter gingerly approaches morality, religion, and theology. For when, after two weeks of work, I was finished with the section, or thought myself finished, I read it to Adorno one evening in my room. He had no objections to make on musical matters, but took issue with the end, the last forty lines, in which after all the darkness, a ray of hope, the possibility of grace, appears. Those lines did not then stand as they stand now; they had gone wrong. I had been too optimistic, too kindly, too pat, had kindled too much light, had been too lavish with the consolation. I had to grant that Adorno's criticisms were justified. The first thing next morning I sat down to a thorough overhauling of the one and a half or two pages, and gave them the circumspect form they now have. Only now, in the rewriting of the passage, did I hit upon the phrases "transcendence of despair", the "miracle that passes belief", and that poetic final cadence, quoted in almost every discussion of the book, about the "voice of mourning" changing its meaning and abiding as a "light in the night".

Christmas 1946 was sultry, with a sky threatening rain. On December 23, still busy with the cantata, I had a vivid recollection of my childhood, for this would be the evening in my parents' home when gifts would be given out, since the Holy Night was reserved for a devout and glorious celebration in my grandmother's house, whose ruins—the façade only standing with empty window sockets—I saw so frequently in pictures nowadays. With the tree already decorated, we listened to Handel's *Messiah* over the radio.

During these days I again read Nietzsche's *Ecce Homo*, obviously in preparation for the final sections of the novel. I also read, after having lost the book for many years, parts of Joël's *Nietzsche und die Romantik*, from which I had learned a great deal as a young man, and a copy of which I now obtained from a book dealer. The Dieterles, just back from Europe, described the misery of shattered Germany, the evil smells of cities and people, and the bitter irony that the SS men being held in camps were leading fairly pleasant lives, taking sunbaths and enjoying the same good rations as the American soldiers.

This Christmas Eve we had to do without the grandchildren. We spoke by telephone with Erika and Klaus in New York, with the children in Mill Valley, with Frido. For our evening concert we listened to the Ninth

Symphony—highly suitable to what I was engaged on. Never had I more deeply admired the scherzo and adagio—but once again could summon up no affection for the variations of disjointed last movement.

I worked on the novel every morning and once again read through Dostoevsky's *The House of the Dead* during the last days of the year. It was a time of heavy rains. The behaviour of the Committee on Un-American Activities, now turning its attention to the patently Communist-plagued Library of Congress, depressed and horrified me. Dr. Hermann Rauschning and his wife came to supper at our house shortly before the end of the year. We talked of politics. In his opinion the Germans as a nation could no longer be tolerated; what would remain were the Germans as individuals. He thought it a good thing to set up some sort of European federation in which the various German states would be included, but with the name of Germany as a whole abandoned.

On the last day of the year, which was fair and windy, I had still not quite finished Chapter XLVI. In the evening Golo came to visit, and brought young Eysoldt, the son of the actress Gertrud Eysoldt, who in my youth had made an ineradicable impression upon me in the part of Wede-kind's Lulu under Reinhardt's direction. The young people asked for a reading, and I read about Adrian's doctors, and from his dialogue with the devil. The conversation after-wards turned upon Hugo Wolf and how (this was new to me) he had visited a bordello just once and had caught the "French" disease from a girl whom his pianist friend there had relinquished to him.

New Year's Day 1947 brought me a true joy. In the morning I had finished the cantata chapter, though this ending was to be revised. A few days before, I had sent

Erika in New York the parts of the manuscript she had not yet seen, about ten chapters, for her to check. Now, upon my return from a walk, I found to my mild alarm an announcement of a telegram "not to be telephoned". It was fetched, and read in English: "Read all night. Shall go into new year reddened eyes but happy heart. Wondering only how on earth you do it. Thanks, congratulations, etc." What a joy to my heart this characteristic utterance of the dear child! I had known, I suppose, that she would weep over Echo. What had happened, as she told me soon afterwards, contained far more of life's comedy than I had imagined. It seemed that after reading all night she had, in honour of the new year, submitted herself to the care of a beauty shop. In the afternoon, while reading the Echo chapter, the whole of her artful make-up, mascara and all, had been washed away by tears and flowed in black streaks over her face.

Then, too, the German edition of *Lotte in Weimar* reached me that day. Not by chance, no doubt, and with my consent, it was the first of my books to be republished in Germany. We spent the evening with the Chaplins, Dieterles, Feuchtwangers and Hanns Eisler at the home of Dr. Weil, the philosopher, and his American wife. With Eisler I once again had one of those talks about Wagner which so amused me, compounded as they were of enthusiasm and malice.

Almost at the same time there arrived a letter, accompanied by documentary enclosures, from Bayreuth. It was from Dr. Franz Beidler, the grandson of Wagner, who in features bore an uncanny resemblance to him. For days I considered the problem presented by this letter. Beidler had left Germany in 1933. I knew him from Berlin and Munich, and later in Zürich he had been a frequent visitor to our

179

house. He had read to us a few times from the opening sections of his book, probably not yet completed, on his grandmother Cosima—a completely critical book, of course. Now the mayor of Bayreuth, concerned for the honour of his city and anxious for a reorganization of the Wagner theatre and a resumption of the festival "in a democratic spirit", had turned to Beidler, who had been in consistent opposition to Hitlerian Bayreuth and to the régime of his aunt. He had offered Beidler the management, and after a long exchange of letters had invited him to come and talk the matter over in Bayreuth. Beidler may have welcomed the trip, I think, for the opportunity it offered to obtain access to the archives of Wahnfried, which had been closed to him, much to the detriment of his book.

There had been negotiations over various details of the mayor's plan, the list of sponsors, the setting up of a board of trustees. Beidler had taken the position that I must be appointed honorary president, and had more or less made his co-operation hinge upon this matter. Now he was writing to me to offer me the post with great earnestness and cordiality. The idea struck me as strange, fantastic, and in a way shocking. For a hundred reasons, intellectual, political, and material, the whole idea appeared utopian, unworldly, and dangerous to me, in part premature, in part obsolete, already outmoded by time and history. I was incapable of taking it seriously. All that I did take seriously were the thoughts, emotions, and memories it stirred in me —memories of my lifelong relationship to the world of Wagner, which had only been inflamed and deepened by my youthful reading of Nietzsche's criticism. I recalled the enormous influence the equivocal magic of this art had had upon my youth—an influence which might even be called determining. The sinister side of this art had been revealed by the role it had played in the Nazi state. Was it now to be restored to its purity (but had it ever been pure?), and was I in the reality of later life to take up an official, representative position in what had been the myth of my youth? It was no temptation, but it was a dream. In truth, I should have been finished earlier with the last fifty pages of *Faustus* if this will-o'-the-wisp had not flitted before me for days, and if I had not been taken up with drafting the evasive, dilatory answer that I felt was the right thing to write to Beidler.

Chapter XLVII, dealing with the gathering of friends and Adrian's confession, had been begun for better or worse on the second day of the new year, and I recall that on the evening of that day I once again heard Schubert's glorious B flat major Trio, and meditated while I listened on the happy state of music that it represented, on the destiny of the musical art since then—a lost paradise. I was also reading Mörike's prose. I was especially impressed, and even roused to envy, by his *Das Stuttgarter Hutzel-männlein* (*The Hobgoblin of Stuttgart*), with its natural and apparently unstudied handling of older German.

One day an advertisment came my way which, quite irrationally, struck me as a wild and monstrous mistake. Oprecht's catalogue arrived from Zürich. There, in clear print, was an announcement of *Faustus*—with its full title and even the probable price for the clothbound edition! I cannot describe the feelings with which I read this announcement—feelings of incredulity, anguish, sheer fright, as at a well-meant but embarrassing indiscretion. Here I was still engaged in the struggle with the book, and in the course of such work one endures to the very last word the notion that crucial difficulties still remain to be overcome and that what has been done stands in need of being

181

rescued by what remains to be done. To see offered as finished goods, bound in cloth, the thing that seemed to me still so unfinished gave me a sense of gruesome prematureness. Moreover, for all that I had been so filled with the book that I had spoken of it freely to members of my circle, the thought of its being offered to the public was still, at the bottom of my soul, alien and incomprehensible to me. The book contained too much of my life, too many of my secrets. With what haste I put the catalogue and its shocking announcement out of sight!

I needed seventeen days for the next-to-last chapter—the last, really, for the end was conceived as an epilogue. Adrian's speech touched me deeply, and came from the heart. Only my old habit of giving political matters equal place beside creative and personal activities, of alternating between these realms, can explain the fact that I still took note of the events of the day, such as Byrnes' resignation as Secretary of State and his replacement by General Marshall, who was called home from China. Nor did my writing down the *oratorio* keep me from paying close attention to news from inside Germany. Ernst Wiechert, a prominent member of the Inner Emigration, was at the time speaking publicly of "this hopeless nation". Although it was not quite clear whether he meant a nation which was being left no hope, or a nation in which it was impossible to place hope, the question was somewhat clarified by his further remark that, if Hitler were to come again today, sixty to eighty per cent of the Germans would receive him with open arms. He did not say that two hopelessnesses were crossing paths, namely, that of the Germans and that of our occupation policy. However, Wiechert has since gone over to the Outer Emigration, taking up residence in Switzerland—from acute displeasure that the authorities were so inconsiderate as to quarter displaced persons on his farm.

Oppressive southerly winds and hot suns, typical *föhn* weather, prevailed during those January days. On one such day, closing the long succession of numbered chapters, I gave to the Bavarian peasant woman—she, too, drawn from real life—the last word, and began my preparations for the epilogue. On the morning of January 29 I wrote the last lines of *Doctor Faustus*, as I had had them framed in my mind for a long time—Zeitblom's silent, fervent prayer for his friend—and looked back over the three years and eight months during which I had lived under the tension of this work, from that May morning in the midst of the war when I had first taken up the pen to begin it. "I am finished," I said to my wife when she fetched me in the car from my usual walk towards the ocean. And she, who had stood by me through many a finishing, how heartily she congratulated me! "With good reason?" the diary asks. And adds: "At least it is a moral accomplishment."

In truth, I did not have the feeling of having finished simply because the words "the end" had been written. "Occupied with the manuscript, reflecting on it and making improvements," was the diary entry for a good many days thereafter. First of all, I cut various items in the epilogue which were found to be too harrowing when I read them aloud. I returned to the violin sonata and the chamber music sections, and tinkered with them. I inserted the Dante motto, and for a while considered the advisability of dividing up the heavy mass of chapters into six "books", thereby giving the whole a clearer form. I had already carried that out; then I let the plan drop again. Another week passed, the first week of February, before I declared the book "finally done with", and vowed not to lay hand on it again. We spent the evening with the Alfred Neumanns and drank champagne to toast the completion of a work to which this good friend had contributed so much. After the coffee I read the Echo chapter. Everyone was much moved. Kitty, so we heard next day, was unable to sleep that night, so strongly was she affected by the death of the child.

Now it was time to do something about the Nietzsche lecture, for my speaking tour to the East and to Europe, for which we were making our first preparations. This took me approximately four weeks. It came to forty manuscript pages, about twenty pages too long for oral delivery, in both English and German. Erika accomplished a masterpiece of editorial work in preparing the essay for the lecture hall. By a hundred deletions of details, yet preserving all the essentials, she cut it exactly in half. An article for Hermann Hesse's seventieth birthday, along with editing the English version of the Nietzsche lecture, occupied me the last weeks before our departure. On April 22 we set out for the East, and on May 11 embarked on the *Queen Elizabeth*. I lectured in London. One June morning—and it was like a dream—I sat on the stage of the Schauspielhaus in Zürich, where eight years ago I had bidden farewell to Europe by reading from *Lotte in Weimar*. Happy and animated by the reunion with this dear city, I performed Fitelberg's Riccaut scene for an audience that helped me celebrate the occasion in the friendliest fashion. We spent several weeks of that sunny summer in Flims, in the Grisons, and there I read daily the proofs of *Doctor Faustus* as they poured in from the printer in Winterthur. The saga of its genesis had ended. That of its earthly life had begun.